Mark Simons
Aquinas College
Grand Rapids, Mich.

Rupp's Championship Basketball

Rupp's

for
Player
Coach
and
Fan

PRENTICE-HALL, INC.

CHAMPIONSHIP
BASKETBALL

Second Edition

Adolph F. Rupp

Englewood Cliffs, N. J.

LIBRARY OF CONGRESS
CATALOG CARD NUMBER 56-13418

Current printing (last digit):

17 16 15 14 13 12 11 10 9

PRINTED IN THE UNITED STATES OF AMERICA

12618—C

To the Memory of

My Mother
Greatest And Best Of All My Teachers

AND TO MY BOYS,
WHEREVER THEY MAY BE, ESPECIALLY

Second Lt. Melvin Charles Brewer,
U. S. Army (Class of '43)
France, August 6, 1944

Captain Kenneth Haynes England,
U. S. Army (Class of '42)
Italy, April 14, 1945

First Lt. James William Goforth,
U. S. Marine Corps (Class of '38)
Saipan, June 22, 1944

Seaman 1/c Walter Marion Johnson,
U. S. Navy (Class of '43)
Pacific, July 30, 1945

Second Lt. James Libern King,
U. S. Army Air Corps (Class of '42)
Germany, February 24, 1944

Key to Charts

   O   Offensive Player

   ✗   Defensive Player

  ⟶   Path of Player

  ⇢   Path of Ball

 〰〰 Dribble

 〰⟲ Pivot

 ⟼   Screen

   R   Rebound

Preface

I am delighted to present to coaches and players a revision of *Rupp's Championship Basketball,* bringing the game up to date in line with all rule changes up to the present time.

Since this book covers a subject in which there is so much change, I necessarily have been reminded of a poem that has come to my desk which I believe illustrates perfectly that, as time goes on, this book too shall pass away. I regret that I do not have the name of the author of this poem, but I should like to leave the thought therein to the readers of this book.

> A mighty monarch in the days of old
> Made offer of high honor, wealth, and gold
> To one who should produce in form concise
> A motto for his guidance, terse, yet wise;
> A precept, soothing in his hours forlorn,
> Yet one that in his prosperous days would warn.
> Many the maxims sent the King, men say,
> **The one he chose . . . "This too shall pass away"!**

This book is written primarily to give to readers, to students and players of the game, an exact picture of basketball as it is played here at the University of Kentucky. The writer has received hundreds of requests during the past few years to write a book on basketball so that coaches might have an exact picture of our style of basketball. The writer also annually receives hundreds of letters requesting information on various phases of the game, and the correspondence necessary to answer all of these requests has become so voluminous that it has taken a great deal of time. It was felt that a book by the author would answer at least a goodly number of these questions.

This book has been written with the purpose of presenting as accurately and briefly as possible the ideas and philosophy that have proved helpful to me as a coach. There is very little new in the game of basketball. The ideas of the game that I have formulated have been the result of many years' experience in the game.

I am grateful to the basketball coaches of America and to my boys, who have taught me many more things than I am able to present in this volume. I am also grateful for the assistance that has been rendered to me in preparing this work. I am especially grateful to Mrs. Louise Gilchrist, who not only has helped to prepare the text but also has aided in the drawing of all the diagrams for the book. I am also grateful to Mrs. Jane B. Rollins, who has taken part in this revision.

If the reader during the season of play should have occasion to refer to this book and find just one thing that will help him solve some problem, then I will consider all the effort in preparing this volume well spent.

ADOLPH F. RUPP

Table of Contents

Medical examination . .	3
Time of practice	4
Equipment	4
Care of the feet	5
Shin splints—pathology	
and treatment	6
Weight	7
Care of nosebleed	
(epistaxis)	7
Colds	7
Staleness	8
Injuries	8
Warm-up drills	9
Visiting teams	10
The coach	10
Cutting the squad	12

1

**Getting Ready
for the Season . .   1**

2

On Watching Basketball:
A Word to the Fan 14

3

Fundamentals 21

Catching the ball	29
Two-handed chest pass .	29
Two-handed bounce pass	29
Two-handed underhand pass . . .	30
One-handed underhand pass . . .	30
Two-handed overhead pass	31
One-handed overhead pass	31
Right and left shoulder pass	31
Hook pass	32
Slap pass or shove pass .	32
Flip pass	32
One-handed roll pass . .	33
The backhand pass . . .	33
Fumbling (causes) . . .	33
Passing hints	34

4

Passing 27

Spot shooting	38
Two-handed push shot . .	40
Two-handed underhand shot . . .	41
Two-handed overhead shot	44
One-handed shots . . .	44
One-handed dribble-in shot	45
One-handed, under the basket shot (right or left)	45
One-handed turn around shot (right or left) . . .	46

5

Shooting 35

Shooting (Cont.)

One-hand, in motion
push shot   46
Set position shot   47
Cross-arm shot, or right or
left shoulder shot . . .   47
Flip shot   47
Tip shot   48
Shooting hints   48

6

Dribbling 50

Dribbling technique . . .   51
Objections to the dribble .   52
Cautions in the use of
the dribble   52

7

Pivoting 54

Reverse pivot   55
Side-line pivot   56
Front or roll pivot   56
Pivoting hints   56

8

**Faking and
Footwork 58**

Footwork   59

9

**Getting Possession
of the Ball . . . 63**

Center-jump   64
Held balls   65
Free balls   65
Rebounds   65

10

Individual Offense 67

11

Screen Plays 70

12

Seven Cardinal Principles of Offensive Play . 77

1. Get the position shot . . 78
2. Get the long shot . . . 79
3. Get the over shot . . . 79
4. Get the second shot . . 80
5. Get the percentage shot 80
6. Take out the floater . . 81
7. Control the ball . . . 82

13

Team Offense . . 84

General principles of
   team play 85
Qualifications of the
   players in team play . . 87
Mechanics of
   the pivot play 90

14

Fast Break 95

Eastern style of play . . . 98
Fast break 100
Hints for offensive teams . 101

15

Offensive Guard Play 102

16

Kentucky's Continuity Offense 119

17

Individual Defense 123

Other defensive hints . . 128
Defensive rebounding . . 132

18

Seven Cardinal Principles of Defensive Play . 133

1. Cut down the number
   of shots 135
2. Cut down the
   percentage of shots . . 136
3. Cut down everything
   under eighteen feet . . 136

Seven Cardinal
Principles of
Defensive Play
(Cont.)

4. Cut down the
   second shots 136
5. Cut down the
   cheap baskets 137
6. Point the ball on all
   long shots 137
7. Prevent the ball from
   going to the pivot . . 137

19

Team Defense,
Man to Man . . 139

Guarding the pivot man . 146
Defense after shot . . . 148
Shifting man-to-man
   defense 150
Sinking man-to-man
   defense 151
Full-court press 152

20

Zone Defense . . . 153

Three-two shifting zone . . 153
Two-one-two shifting zone . 154
Two-three shifting zone . . 155
One-two-two shifting zone . 156
Two-two-one shifting zone . 157
Strong points of the
   zone defense 158
Weaknesses of the
   zone defense 159

21

Defense Against
the Fast Break . 160

Defense against the
   fast break 161
Switching 163
Freezing or stalling . . . 165
Smothering, sandwiching,
   or two-timing 166

22

Substituting and
Time Out 170

When to make
   substitutions 170
Calling time out 172

23

Organization on Trips 174

24

Tournament Play 178

25

The Practice Week 181

26

Diet and

Training Table . 184

Meats and poultry . . .	185
Vegetables	186
Fruits	186
Breads	186
Beverages	186
Menu—game day (game 8:00 p.m.) . . .	186
Miscellaneous	188

27

Duties of a Manager 189

28

A Coach's Relationship to His Team . . . 192

29

Scouting 197

30

Final Hints and Special Drills 201

Index 215

1

Getting Ready for the Season

If championship class basketball is to be played, then we feel that a team must be properly conditioned. Conditioning means getting the players prepared for forty minutes of hard basketball by the time the season opens and then maintaining this condition for the remainder of the schedule. Some teams are never in good condition due to lack of work, while other teams are overworked. A team must have both physical and mental conditioning; they work hand in hand.

Conditioning means training. Training should be by tradition rather than by orders. Some schools are able to develop good training habits and a high morale or spirit. A winning team will develop these. Early in the year I have a frank talk with my squad. I talk along these lines: "This is your team, not mine. I am not going to lay down a set of rules and training requirements. I haven't the time or the desire to check on you in order to enforce them. I am not a policeman; what results we accomplish this year in a large measure will depend on what you boys desire to do. Championships are not won by wishing and by hope. They are won by hard work and a willingness on the part of the boys to sacrifice some of the normal phases of college life. If you are in the habit of smoking, I would like you to stop. Let your opponents smoke. Let us make it a rule to be in bed by 10:30 or at least off the street and in our rooms. I know that some of you must study late. But don't waste your time. We have had many championship teams here at Kentucky before, and the faculty, students, and alumni expect you to follow in their path. Many boys have made All American and All Conference honors on this floor. Kentucky is rich in basketball tradition. Are you willing to work and sacrifice to add to this? It is your team, you make the rules."

If a group of boys are instilled with the desire to win, then the physical conditioning is not difficult. A coach may have a difficult problem when he has a long, tough schedule with a tournament at the close of the season. It may be desirable in conditioning the boys not to try for peak condition at the beginning of the season. However, in recent years, we have had several outstanding national tournaments in collegiate play and if your team is to qualify for these it is essential to have a good "won and lost" record. Therefore, a coach must win even the early December games. It makes a difficult problem as the team must be up for fully four months of play. Conditioning, therefore, is a season-long procedure. Since it is hard to keep a team on razor edge for such a long period of time, it is necessary to use the practice period intelligently and not overwork the boys. It may be necessary to give the players several days' rest during the week to insure their being in proper condition to play a full game at maximum efficiency. It is also necessary to be sure that you are teaching your players properly and that you are getting the maximum use of your material. Good coaching of good material and proper conditioning should bring championship play.

Every coach should have a definite plan and every practice session should have an aim and purpose. If every practice is well organized and the boys see the reason for doing the work, they will not only do it well but they will do it with enthusiasm. The road to anywhere is filled with pitfalls, and it takes a man of character and determination not to fall into them. If you see a man on top of a mountain, he didn't light there—chances are he had to climb. And if you see a man on top in his profession, chances are that he worked with a definite plan, aim, and purpose in mind. Any man that is successful will naturally be envied by those less successful. However, I think that possibly the following excerpt from Pakenham Beatty's "Self Reliance" contains a good philosophy for every coach:

> By your own soul learn to live,
> And if men thwart you, take no heed,
> If men hate you, have no care;
> Sing your song, dream your dream, hope
> your hope and pray your prayer.

If you will follow this philosophy of life I am sure that you will be successful. It will create in your team an intangible, mysterious element that is known as *spirit*. Spirit is what enables a player to do better than he is physically capable of doing. How is spirit developed? Here at the University our teams have a tremendous tradition of success. It is not necessary for us to do a big selling job to our boys. Spirit is contagious; and, if we can create within the boys that genuine desire to give the best that they have, then we are sure that the best will come back to us. We do not wish merely to *participate* in sports, we wish to become *successful* in sports. And, if we can create within the boys that intense desire to win—to win fairly and by the rules, to win gracefully—then we feel that we have taught a boy a fine philosophy of life. You usually hear whenever you have a losing season that "we are building character." We feel the finest character is being built when we have a winning team and when we teach our boys to be successful in all their undertakings. We believe that success in sports has a carry-over value for success in other undertakings.

Medical examination

It is extremely desirable that every boy who reports for basketball should do so only after he has a careful medical examination.

In many schools the children are given periodic medical examinations from the first grade on, and their health records are carried with them until they graduate from high school. If this information is available for college coaches it will prove helpful.

A boy should be checked carefully for hernia. His lungs, heart, teeth, eyes, nose, throat, blood pressure, and feet should be checked. If the tonsils are diseased they should be removed. Foot defects can often be corrected by prescribing proper shoes. It is also well to check the medical examination record to see what vaccinations a boy has had. We here at the University of Kentucky have found the new type of flu shots very desirable. No coach cares to use a boy in basketball if the competition should prove harmful to the boy. The only way to be sure of this is to require a medical examination. That also protects the coach in his work.

Time of practice

The best time to practice is in the afternoon after class work has been completed. We start our practice here at the University of Kentucky at 3:30 and continue until 5:00 or 5:30, depending on the work that must be done on that particular day. Afternoon practice enables the players to eat their regular meals and permits them to spend the evenings in study. It also allows the players to relax before going to bed and allows them to get from 8 to 10 hours sleep. However, it is desirable before the season's play begins to practice several times at night in order to accustom the players to game conditions and to game time.

Equipment

Far too often schools neglect practice equipment and spend all of their money for classy game uniforms. However, practice equipment is important because a boy will use it fully twenty-five times more than he will his game equipment. I believe that basketball should teach health and cleanliness and this cannot be done if a boy is required to practice in dirty equipment. This practice equipment need not be expensive, but a boy should have a clean change of practice equipment each day. Be sure that the socks are soft and that they fit properly. Sometimes it is desirable to use a light inner-sock. We always have sweat suits, especially the shirts, on the sideline and the minute a boy is removed from play he is required to put on this sweat equipment. This prevents the boys from taking colds.

Care of the feet

Watch the feet carefully in the first week of practice. Carelessness during this period can injure your team. If the feet begin to burn, allow the players to drop from the regular work and spend the time on things that will not cause injury to the feet, such as free throwing, etc. Toughen the feet by using a compound of tincture of benzoin or tannic acid and have the players dry their feet between the toes to prevent "athlete's foot."

Athlete's foot. This skin ailment is caused by a fungus growth which thrives in a damp, hot environment. So far as is known, fungi do not die a natural death. They have been known to survive twenty-five years in a dried state, then suddenly burst out in full bloom. Prevention is the best cure. Issue clean socks each day. Be sure to dry between the toes. Use a moisture-absorbing fungicidal powder after drying the feet well. In many cases shoes should be dusted daily with foot powder. There are many remedies for the treatment of athlete's foot. We have found Whitfield's ointment, or 8 per cent salicylic acid the best for minor cases. For the more advanced cases a twenty-minute soaking of the feet in potassium permanganate solution is a near sure cure. Use two 5-grain tablets in a half gallon of warm water.

Blisters. As a rule open the blister with a sterile scalpel, paint with tincture of benzoin (Merthiolate or Nitrotan), and fill the blister capsule with sulfa granules. Place the skin flap back in place and cover with sterile gauze. Place over this a doughnut of moleskin to eliminate pressure and irritation. This also enables air to reach the enclosed parts.

Floor burns. Wash all floor burns with athletic soap or hydrogen peroxide and apply a compress using Nitrotan or furacin benzoin. If an infection should develop, then use a sulfa ointment.

Ankles. Some coaches prefer that all players use muslin or webbing ankle wraps in practice and in a game. This is a good precaution and will help prevent sprains. If sprains should occur apply cold packs, ice, or cold water, immediately. Use this treatment for at least 30 minutes or until you are sure that there will be no more swelling. Then tape the ankle tightly. As soon as the player is able he should exercise this ankle and start on corrective resistance exercises. Remove the tape each day and put on new tape. It is a wise precaution to continue to wrap the injured ankle for the remainder of the season. All serious sprains should be X-rayed. Excellent results have been obtained through drug therapy (alidase, wydase, trypsin, etc.)—suggest you talk this over with your team physician.

Shin splints — pathology and treatment

There are several conflicting ideas concerning the pathology of this condition. However, we will cover the most common type, which is irritation to the interosseous membrane. This membrane is located between the tibia and fibula (large and small) bones. Its functions are many: It serves as a shock absorber and supporting structure between the tibia and fibula. It serves as an "elastic bone" to which at least six anterior muscles and three posterior muscles have attachments. These two groups of muscles are antagonistic in that the anterior group of muscles are primarily flexors, that is, they pull up and invert the foot (turn the foot to the inside) and extend the toes (straighten and turn the toes up). The posterior group of muscles are primarily extensors, that is, they extend (raise) the heel, invert the foot (turn the foot outward), and flex the toes (turn them downward).

When we take into consideration the terrific stretching, pulling, jerking, and straining the interosseous membrane is subjected to, we can readily understand how susceptible it is to irritation. This membrane has very poor circulation; and when it becomes irritated, this irritation spreads to the surrounding muscular area.

Treatment. Since the anterior group of muscles have a tendency to warm up slowly and cool off quickly, continuous heat and rest is prescribed. Shin splints respond to low heat, shortwave diathermy, steam packs, or whirlpool (106°–190°), followed by overnight analgesic packs.

Taping. Place a piece of sponge about one-fourth of an inch thick in the heel of the shoe. In severe cases tape the arch and shin as follows: To tape the *arch,* start a one-inch strip of tape on top of the foot at the base of the little toe. Bring the tape from outside to inside across the longitudinal arch, keeping steady pressure; hook around the heel and continue along lateral side of foot to starting point. Start the next strip on top of the foot at the base of the big toe, bring the tape across the arch of the foot, hook around the heel, and continue along the medial side to the starting point. Place an anchor strip around the foot at the base of the toes.

To tape the *shin,* place a strip of sponge rubber, two to four inches wide and four to six inches long, over the shin area and tape firmly with even pressure. An elastic tape or elastic bandage is preferred.

Sore feet. Use boric acid, talcum powder, tannic acid, or tincture of benzoin. All are good.

Weight

It is desirable to keep a weight chart. At the beginning of the practice sessions a player will lose weight but after several weeks, a player should not progressively lose weight. After the player is in condition his weight should fluctuate very little.

Care of nosebleed (epistaxis)

The treatment of nosebleed is fairly standardized throughout the world. First, determine the cause and extent of injury (concussion, contusion, etc.). If nosebleed is caused from a contusion, (1) Place patient in supine position. (2) Use cotton or gauze rolled to about one-half to one inch long, saturate with a hematischetic solution, such as adrenalin, and insert these plugs into the nasal passages. This is usually sufficient and the athlete can resume play. In a severe hemorrhage the same procedure should be used, except that ice packs should be applied to the nose and facial area and at the base of the skull to slow down circulation.

If the hemorrhage continues and drips into the throat, have the patient refrain from swallowing it. The serum in the blood will often cause upset stomach.

Colds

We prefer to have the temperature of our gymnasium between 50 and 60 degrees for all practice sessions and all games. Flu shots and cold shots are advisable. We use vitamin pills also. It is easier to prevent colds than to try to cure them. Be sure that the players understand that their heads should be dry and covered before they go out into the winter cold. Have the players taper off in their showers so that they finish with a cold one. Advise them to rub dry and not to go out in cold weather immediately after showers.

Staleness

Watch for staleness if you have a long and hard schedule. There are several signs that will tip off the coach in regard to this. It may be a loss of weight, a lack of enthusiasm in practice, irritability of the players, or a lack of power to finish a game in strong condition. Staleness may be due to overwork, too much study, too much outside work, lack of sleep, or examinations. The best treatment is complete rest and a change in diet. Keep the boys away from the gymnasium for several days. Allow them to get more sleep. Sleep is the master builder of our bodies.

Injuries

Injuries in basketball will usually consist of a sprained ankle, a bruised elbow, a sprained wrist, a Charley horse in the thigh muscle, or a jammed finger. We keep a bucket of ice water on our practice floor every day, and as soon as we get a sprain we immediately place the sprained ankle or hand in this cold water and leave it there for at least 30 minutes. The ankle is then taped and, if it is a severe sprain, the boy is taken to the infirmary and an X ray is made. If the X ray shows that no bones are broken, the ankle then is treated by our trainer. It is well for every athletic coach to have a team physician in whom he has complete confidence. There will always be someone in every town who has a knowledge of athletic injuries and the method by which they should be treated. He will be glad to work with the trainer on every injury and good results can be accomplished in this way. The next day after a boy sprains his ankle we apply heat for about 30 minutes by means of a whirlpool. We have found this so satisfactory that we have installed five whirlpools in our Coliseum and three in our football training room on the practice field. After this treatment, if the sprain is not too severe, the boy is permitted to work on it. If it is severe, he will stay off of it for another day. This much is true of a sprained ankle: during the night the injury will not permit relaxation in that area and the next morning there will be a slight stiffness. The nerve stimulus and blood circulation are retarded either by swelling or disuse. The whirlpool will tend to warm up that part of the body, and it may be that this will relax the ankle.

We like to get to these injuries immediately. We consider every boy valuable to our team. One small injury or bruise can wreck an athlete, a system of plays, and possibly a whole season. There is no excuse for neglect and a boy should be attended to immediately.

A good trainer is invaluable and it is the attention that he gives to these small things that can often mean the difference in your season. For high schools that cannot afford to hire a competent trainer, I would like to suggest that their coaches make it a part of their training to spend at least a few days each year at a coaching clinic and work carefully with the trainers assigned there. Hundreds of high school athletes come here every year to make use of our training facilities and to consult our trainer. I have heard many coaches say that the help that they have received here in getting their boys ready to play has meant a great deal to them. An injured boy should never be used until he is able to play. That should be a part of every program: *Safety in Sports.*

Warm-up drills

Some coaches may use warm-up drills or setting-up exercises. This is not necessary if the fundamental drills are properly organized. A boy will naturally warm up properly with the shooting drills. However, if any of the players have individual weaknesses, it may be desirable to use drills for those cases. In order to develop leg muscles, it may be desirable to use jumping ropes. To develop the arms and fingers use a small rubber ball that fits comfortably in the hand and squeeze it hard. Use the push-up exercises, placing the finger tips in a cupped position on the floor as a support. Many coaches recommend a medicine ball, which we have found to be excellent.

Visiting teams

At Kentucky we treat our visiting teams as we would like to be treated ourselves. There are four visitors' dressing rooms, all of which are identical to our own, containing large rest rooms, shower rooms, and locker areas. We make it a policy to offer our training room facilities and the services of our trainer and team physician. If our visiting team does not have a student manager, we furnish one to take care of their water, towels, and equipment. This trend has spread rapidly throughout the South.

The coach

The coach should be in uniform at all times, and if possible should aid in demonstration. All of the players should be carefully checked from the time practice begins and playing faults should be corrected immediately. The coach should be on the floor to help with all these problems. This determines his teaching ability. The practice session should be closed to outsiders, for it is often necessary to criticize the players and they may be sensitive if spectators are present.

If the coach is determined to stay in the coaching profession, he will develop from year to year. This much is true: no coach has a monopoly on the knowledge of basketball. There are no secrets in the game. The only secrets, if there are any, are good teaching of sound fundamentals, intelligent handling of men, a sound system of play, and the ability to instill in the boys a desire to win. As a coach advances from year to year he will, by experience, find out the things that are good and that should be stressed, and the things that are not so good and should be either eliminated or neglected.

The way a coach develops in his career is like the story of a well known sports writer of today. One of his first assignments was to cover the Sugar Bowl game in New Orleans. He was so thrilled with the game that he failed to take any notes and after the game was over, was faced with the necessity of writing a story for his paper. While all the other newspapermen were pecking away at their typewriters, try as he would, he couldn't think of a way to start his story. Finally he turned to the sports writer next to him, who was busy trying to meet his deadline, hoping to get some suggestions. He said, "A good game wasn't it?" The reply was, "Yeah." That didn't help him a great deal so in a few minutes he said, "A nice day, wasn't it?" Again he got the same reply. In a few moments he led off with this question, "A beautiful sunset, isn't it?" And again the same reply. Finally he said, "It's in the west, isn't it?" Immediately he received this as an answer. "Well, son, if it isn't you have the biggest scoop in the history of the world." He finally wrote his story and today, after years of experience, is one of America's best sports writers.

The purpose of this story is merely to point out to young coaches the fact that they will enlarge their experience as the years roll by and coaching will become an easier task. A coach should be patient in his teaching and remember this one thing: you cannot teach everything in one day. It takes hours and hours of repetition in drills, in plays, and in fundamentals, to develop the coordination and the timing that one desires.

A coach should be a good judge of material and he should be able to develop in it versatility. That is, he should develop the boys so that they may be able to play in more than one position. It is also the coach's responsibility when he has good material not to overcoach or ruin it, but to get the absolute maximum out of the abilities of the boys. A coach should understand human nature as well as the specific attitudes, interests, inclinations, and desires of the boys that he is coaching. He should be able to instill in these boys the willingness to learn and the desire to win. He should develop pride in these boys so that they will understand that it is not only a privilege to be able to play the game of basketball, but that it is also a responsibility. A coach should be able to develop a plan of play and then be able to carry it out for the entire year. A coach should plan early in his career to decide on a system of play and then to develop the maximum number of variations from it to suit his material. There will be boys on his squad in some years who, due to their ability, will be able to carry out some plays better than others. We have such players here at the University of Kentucky every year. We like to think of our guards as quarterbacks, as they are required to start the plays. Some of our boys will be able to run some of our plays better than others, and whether it is due to the fact that they are more successful in doing so, or for some other reason, they like to run the plays that bring about a score.

A coach should be able to substitute intelligently, for after the game begins it is in the hands of the coach. If a boy makes a mistake, if he fails to cash in on his opportunities, if the players have been assigned wrongly—it is up to the coach to substitute instantly and correct the mistakes. It is by means of substitution of players that a coach can control the game.

A coach should not choose his men for the team in the first few weeks of play. Give all of the boys a chance of making the team and don't play favorites. Although many of our outstanding athletes today are small, if possible choose big men. It is well to have a big guard for defensive rebounding purposes. It is also well to have for forwards tall boys who can tip in rebounds. Naturally, in our style of play we like to have a big, rangy center with good coordination, with good reflexes, and who can control the boards. Get good high-spirited boys, for they are the ones that will respond in critical times.

Choose the players for the position that you want them to play and then specialize on their training. We here at Kentucky say that we play "spot" basketball. In other words, we want boys to specialize in certain details if they play in certain positions. Defensively we assign the men in a game and not the positions.

Cutting the squad

We here at the University of Kentucky have decided that it is best not to work the boys too hard the first week of practice. In fact, we usually have about one week of practice that has very little organization. We use a few drills in passing, but most of the time is spent on shooting; for we definitely believe that this practice should never be neglected. We always have a large squad reporting for the team. When it is obvious that players do not possess the ability to make the team, it is a waste of their time and the coach's time to retain them on the squad. It is very easy for us to eliminate at least 50 per cent of the material in the first two days. By the end of the week, we can fairly well choose the material that we wish to keep on for the squad. Naturally some of the boys will be cut off as the weeks go by when it becomes obvious that they are not the type of material for a championship team. We do not believe in having a big squad. We like to keep a squad down to 16 to 20 men, and we like to work these men into a definite pattern of play and teach them the fundamentals as we wish them to be executed. After the squad has been selected be sure to check on the eligibility of all of the players. Do not waste your time on an ineligible man unless he can make up his work and become eligible for the second semester.

Early-season practice should be devoted to fundamental drills. In the second week we begin to put in fundamental drills that will work into our general system of floor play. As the practice goes on we like to select a team that will be composed of eight men that we call our first team. Boys playing together learn to know each other. We believe that good teamwork comes only if the boys learn to work and play together. By having eight good men, we can make frequent substitutions if necessary without demoralizing organized team play.

As the season unfolds you will naturally have more and more scrimmage. See that these practice scrimmages are well officiated and that the players learn the rules. Require that the managers study the rules for they are usually called upon to do this officiating. Look for the boys who have a competitive instinct, who are aggressive, who have courage, and who have a spirit of sacrifice. These are the boys that will respond when the "heat" is on.

2

On Watching Basketball:
A Word to the Fan

In recent years basketball has become America's leading spectator sport. At a conservative estimate, over 100 million people attend basketball games every winter. We can safely assume that a great majority of these enthusiastic spectators know comparatively little about the finer points of the game. As a rule the constant speed and thrills of the sport are enough to satisfy them. But if the fan would take a little time to learn more about the game it would bring him even more thrills than it has in the past.

Unlike football and other bruising sports there is never a let-up in basketball. Once the action starts it is constant except for whistles for out-of-bounds plays and fouls. For this reason many spectators and even some sports writers seem to think that basketball is a game in which ten boys, scantily clad, run up and down the floor untiringly in an attempt to shoot a ball through a suspended net.

In reality basketball is a highly organized game with recognized systems of play comparable to those of football. In football we have the single-wing, the T formation, the split T, and so on. Whereas these football systems are more or less standardized throughout the country, basketball styles of play as a rule are controlled by the geographic locations of the teams using them.

In the East, for example, the game most widely played is the "give-and-go" game. It is a variation of the so-called "pro style" perfected by the Original Celtics of New York City. This style is still employed by most of today's professional teams of the N.B.A. It calls for fine ball handling and lends itself well to free-lancing or "situation" basketball. Each player is usually capable of playing "in" or "out," and the basic move is one in which the ball-handler will pass off (give), then screen for the receiver, and, finally, after momentarily screening, "go" for the basket, usually getting a return pass. LaSalle, Temple, and Holy Cross are leading exponents of his type of game.

In watching various college games, the fan will note that the Southern and Midwestern schools play a rugged game with the accent on body contact and a maximum stress on the offensive side of basketball. These schools feature the controlled fast-break game, which simply means that they fast break whenever the opportunity presents itself. On the other hand, when there is no fast-break situation, they establish either the single or double post and run basic plays in which their pivot men are the focal points in the attack.

Kentucky, Alabama, Dayton, St. Louis, and Iowa are teams which have utilized this type of attack successfully.

Since basketball went big-time with the advent of double-header programs in public arenas in the thirties, coaches from various sections of the country have adopted the finer points of sectional basketball from outstanding quintets of other areas. For example, the one-hand shot and the jump shot are now used in every section of the country. The two-hand set shot is becoming almost as extinct as the Model T Ford, although we still like it at Kentucky.

In the Far West and in the Rocky Mountain area control basketball is typical. Clever ball handling, a minimum of shooting, and then taking only the good percentage shot is the mainspring of the offense. San Francisco and Oklahoma A. & M. are the leading exponents.

Despite this educational process among the coaches which has been going on in the past decade or more, the fan should still recognize sectional playing highlights of the various districts involved. In speaking of defensive basketball we assume that there are four basic styles. The most commonly employed basketball defense is the man-to-man style. This was adopted by Dr. James Naismith, inventor of the game, who wrote "When on the defense stick to your man like glue." Approximately seventy per cent of the teams playing basketball employ this type of defense. In the zone defenses, as the name implies, each player on the defending team is responsible for a certain zone and plays the ball in his assigned territory. When an opponent enters a player's particular zone that player is responsible for the man until he leaves the zone —irrespective of his opponent's size, speed and other abilities. The key words of zone defense are "Watch the ball."

In watching for the zone defense the observer should understand that there are different types. These types are the 3-2, the 2-3, and the 2-1-2. Different variations of these zones may be seen employed by some coaches. All are distinguished by ranging the players in line across the court and assigning certain territories to each player.

The third type of defense is usually termed the screen-switch. This defense is employed when two offensive players crisscross in front of their defensive opponents. It was originated by the late Dr. George Keogan of Notre Dame.

The fourth type of defense is the zone press. Penn State is generally credited with the development of this defense. Many teams today are effectively using the zone press, which is a full-court version of the zone. It is usually employed when behind, when you lack respect for your opponent's ball handling, or when you are playing a slow, deliberate ball-control opponent and you wish to speed up the tempo and thereby upset the timing of your opponent's attack.

Now that you know the types of defense employed it might be a good idea to see how coaches attack these defenses. We can safely assume that ninety per cent of all teams use the quick-break action in any kind of defense. This means that a team drives down the court full speed upon securing possession of the ball. The strategy here is to beat the defense down the court and score before the defense can get organized. Coach Ward Lambert, formerly of Purdue University, always favored this attack whether or not the opposition had set up its defense.

When I first started coaching at the University of Kentucky, the famous Original Celtics basketball team played in our part of the country every winter. They had developed a play that today is the backbone of basketball. I am referring to the "post" or "pivot" play. Dutch Dehnert, a big broad-shouldered individual, used to station himself on the foul line with his back to the hoop. His teammates would pass the ball to him and cut toward him, trying to lead their opponents into a screen in order to break through. The Celtics used the pivot player as a play maker. Today many college coaches station their tallest man under the basket in order to employ his height as a security measure. This big fellow under the basket is more concerned in scoring himself than setting up a play in the style that the Celtics did.

In the style of play that is used by most of the coaches today, we station one big man, the pivot man, in the area near the basket. The two forwards line up on the sides and we allow two men designated as the guards to bring the ball down the floor. Then, by means of well-designed plays that make use of the screen, we try to release one or more players for an unmolested shot at the basket. We usually do this by passing the ball to the pivot man, he in turn passing out to the man who has been freed. The two forwards on the side of the floor are then in excellent position for rebounding in case the basket should be missed, or they in turn can fall back on defense if the basket is made. Frequently in our style of play, you will see our two forwards alternate with our post man in the pivot position. In other words, they will try to take into the pivot a defensive man who is not familiar with guarding a pivot man.

Kentucky has been fortunate in recent years in having outstanding shooters like Watson, Ramsey, and Hatton. When our big men could not shake loose for good pivot shots, they threw the ball out to our smaller men who took shots from very close to mid-court.

No matter how good your team is on defense and offense it is necessary to develop a proper game strategy for each game. This strategy is pointed out by notes gathered from thorough scouting of what the other team has in the line of players, plays, ability and strength. Scouting plays a very important part in basketball as it does in football. By scouting we learn how to utilize our players in an effort to capitalize on what we believe are the weaknesses of our opponents. Many times too we have to utilize our players in such a way as to capitalize on the strength of our opposition.

On January 5, 1952, we were playing L.S.U. in Lexington. Our scouting reports indicated that we would have considerable trouble rebounding against their two big men, Pettit (six feet, nine inches) and Johnson (six feet, ten inches). In making our defensive assignments we were forced to assign Tsioropoulos (six feet, five inches) to Pettit and Hagan (six feet, four inches) to Johnson. Our strategy was to take only the good percentage shots thereby reducing the number of rebounds.

We planned well but could not hit. At the end of the first quarter we were trailing by 11 points. Our scoring reports had also led us to believe that we could successfully employ a full-court press, making it extremely difficult for L.S.U. to get the ball in to their two big men. During the time-out we substituted our fast boys, Evans and Whitaker, with instructions to press all over the court. Our press was so successful that at the end of the third quarter we were enjoying a comfortable 13-point lead. Again our scouting had paid off by enabling us to plan our strategy well in advance of the actual game.

Many times strategy backfires. Do not forget that the other coaches are thinking and striving to pull off a few tricks of their own. I am reminded of a game in 1940 between Duquesne and Long Island University in Madison Square Garden. Coach Clair Bee of Long Island University had scouted Duquesne thoroughly in Pittsburgh prior to the game. He noticed that Moe Becker was the Dukes' high scorer and a great set shooter. When Bee returned to his team he instructed them in how he wanted Becker played.

He was under the assumption, of course, that Becker would continue to shoot from outside as he had done in previous games. When the two teams finally met at the Garden, Becker busied himself setting up shots and plays for his team mate Paul Widowitz, who led the Duquesne team to the eventual triumph over Long Island University. Becker and Widowitz had exchanged roles for the evening. The former became the play maker while the latter assumed the role of shooter. In this instance the scouting backfired.

In 1948 these same two teams met on the Madison Square Garden court. Coach Bee again traveled to Pittsburgh to scout the Dukes. He happened to catch them in a game with Seton Hall in which the Smoky City edged out the New Jersey visiting team in a hotly waged contest. Bee noted one thing which stood his team in good stead when the game was played on the Garden court. He saw that the Duquesne big men drove under the board all night to score. The whole offensive was designed to score from underneath. This was a sharp deviation from Duquesne's style of operation in previous years. Bee reasoned with good logic that the Dukes lacked set players who could score on set shots from outside. Consequently he never had to stop the Dukes from scoring at long range. When the two clubs finally met, Long Island University dropped back on defense and blocked the area underneath the basket, and as a result Duquesne fell a rather easy prey to the Black Birds.

A good deal of the game is played right on the players' bench. The players' bench, you will note, is a beehive of activity. After you acquaint yourself with the fundamentals of the game you can almost surmise what a coach will do in a given circumstance.

If a defensive or offensive isn't working too well, you will notice the coach talking to a group of substitutes next to him on the bench. When the proper moment arises these substitutes are instructed to change the defense or offense. If their new style of operation holds up successfully you can expect the regulars to return to their positions with instructions to use this new style.

When you go to a game it is advisable to buy a program in order to learn as much as possible about the players you are to see. Notice their heights. Try to figure out which are the board men and which the play makers. Learn their numbers and positions; look over the substitute list, and most of all keep score. You can get a great kick out of checking your individual and team score card with the official score which appears in the morning paper.

In order to judge the individual merits of a player learn to ask yourself the following questions: Is he a team player? Does he screen well? Does he set up shots well? Can he shoot from outside? Is he a right-handed shooter or a left-handed shooter? When you begin to look for the answers to these questions you are really enjoying basketball to the utmost. Always remember that basketball is a game of the moment. The players have to deal with situations as they arise and it is fascinating to see how individual players react to given situations. If you will remember some of the fundamentals I have outlined above I am certain that basketball will be even more enjoyable to you in the future than it has been in the past.

3

Fundamentals

Systems of play and styles of offense and defense do not win championships. As mentioned in the first chapter, a coach should decide early in his career on a general system of play. This, of course, can be varied as conditions require.

If there were a secret in successful basketball, then that secret would be drilling on fundamentals. It is unfortunate, however, that many coaches never seem to realize this. Far too often, the entire practice period is spent on goal shooting and scrimmage. The team is not prepared to scrimmage because it has not mastered the fundamental details, and a ragged and rugged afternoon is the result.

I have noticed in the coaching schools throughout the country that whenever the lecturer talks about fundamental drills, he does not command a great deal of attention. However, the minute that he takes a piece of chalk and starts diagramming a play on the blackboard, almost every listener will pull out a pencil and start taking notes. Plays are important, but if the players have not mastered the fundamentals they will never be able to execute the plays. The style of play is not important; almost every coach has a different idea as to the system that should be employed.

Early season practice should be devoted to fundamentals. They establish individual rather than team skill, and enable a coach to attain uniformity in his play. Too much time should not be spent on a single fundamental drill. Have several of these in an afternoon. We always run our guard offense fundamental drill, and our boys really enjoy this. The attitude of the players toward these drills will in a large measure influence their ability to execute them successfully. We have used these drills for many years and in them we have virtually all of the offensive movements that a basketball player requires. When we start these drills, our boys shout and yell constantly. They count the number of consecutive goals that are made and a loud roar goes up from all of them when one is missed. It teaches pride, and I cannot overemphasize this in the building of an athlete. If an athlete has confidence in his ability to execute fundamentals it will give him poise on the floor. It will make him feel that he will be able to take command of any situation that will arise. "As a man thinketh, so is he also," may be applied to the player who plays the game of basketball.

Possibly it seems unusual to the average individual when I say that we spend three-fourths of our practice periods working on fundamentals. Mastery of detail in passing, dribbling, running, faking, pivoting, cutting, rebounding, and footwork is essential to a good basketball player. Regardless of what theories of play you have, unless those theories can be put into actual play by well executed fundamentals, you will fail to have a winning club. Many boys come to us highly recommended but each and every one of them must spend hours of patient work in order to gain the polish required in our type of play. It is a mistake to train a boy in the fine points of the game if he cannot properly execute the fundamental details.

Perhaps the biggest job that faces a basketball coach is in the drilling that he must do in order to get self-control in his men, and in the suppression of individualism in the interest of team play. Basketball surpasses all college games in the matter of teamwork, for in basketball every player on the team receives the ball continually during an offensive movement within the scoring zone. Naturally, at times a boy who does not fit well into an unselfish system of play will tend to monopolize certain phases of the game. He may dribble too much and thereby destroy teamwork. He may shoot when the opportunity is not most favorable and thus seek individual glory rather than team harmony.

In order to build a real machine you must immediately break up this desire for individual glory; you must break up this individual effort. This can best be done by demanding that all players execute the fundamentals of play as required.

Far too often a game of basketball is merely ten players each operating individually. The best illustration of this is the All-Star games at the close of the year in which boys from every section of the country who have had little practice together are brought in to build a team. There is very little harmony in the play and each player, as he gains possession of the ball, will usually try for individual glory rather than for a cooperative offense. It is sometimes possible to build a team with individual stars but this team will never be of championship caliber and will never win the top ball games. A good team must have plays, and plays are executed by means of fundamentals.

Basketball today, in order to present an interesting performance for spectators, must have clever plays. There should be no guesswork about them. They should be planned so that every man knows what to do every moment, and the players should be able to run through the plays in machinelike fashion. Every coach should spend a lot of time building an offense by means of plays, for he should capitalize on positive ball possession. There is nothing more pitiful than a team without effective ammunition trying to penetrate a rugged defense.

Another feature commonly overlooked in basketball is team drilling for the physical requirements of the game. You need speedy footwork, leg spring, and endurance. Give the players such exercises as will develop these. In the early part of the season, it is well to have a set of exercises that you use regularly. Have some skipping ropes and require each player to use them for five minutes each day. Teach them to play on their toes and develop through the use of the skipping rope such leg spring as they will need in a game. Above everything else, do not overwork your men in these early practice sessions. Rather, give them less work than they seem willing to do. Remember one thing, fatigue is cumulative. If you practice until the men are tired and then keep on driving them you are only teaching them bad habits—habits of loafing. They will soon catch on and not give one hundred per cent of their ability because they will be uncertain as to how long the drill will last. They will grow to hate these practice sessions. Furthermore, when they get to the closing moments of a game, they won't have the reserve energy to put on a drive that will lead them to victory.

In a very close game where both teams battle furiously, it is only a question of time until one of them cracks under the pressure. The team that hasn't the reserve energy, that is not playing on its toes, that is not alert, is the team that will crack. Therefore, condition your men so that they will always have sufficient stamina to put across a victory if called upon to do so in the closing minutes of a game. You can't drive a man into condition; it just can't be done. You don't condition the motor of your new automobile by running it wide open the first few weeks, and you don't drive a race horse in the first few weeks at top speed. Both must be gradually broken in. A man's makeup is far more delicate than that of a motor or a horse.

After the season is well advanced it is possible to shorten these fundamental drills and add a scrimmage period. However, it is advisable never to have a scrimmage period after you have had a fundamental defensive drill. It makes the boys defensive-minded and as sure as you try it, you will find that your offensive scrimmage will lose polish. We are firmly convinced that the work that you do during the week pays off in the game on Saturday night. The fundamental drills that you work on in practice will largely determine how your team will react under fire. If you concentrate entirely on offensive fundamentals during the week and neglect the defensive fundamentals, your team will not be ready to play a good defensive game. However, if you work a lot on defensive drills during a particular week, it will pay off in the next game.

Fundamentals, the basic actions of basketball, are the keys to success. The coach who has a magic formula is the one who has mastered the key fundamentals. The magic formula is reached only by hard work and repetition. Countless experiences and persistence will ultimately determine which basic actions on the part of players will enable them to achieve the best possible results with a minimum of wasted time, motion, and effort. Success in basketball has no royal road. The proper execution of plays has a somewhat demoralizing effect on opponents. A team well schooled in fundamentals and in executing plays can often defeat a much more individually talented team.

Keep away from frills. They merely overburden your offensive. Boys can absorb only so much, and if you continue to give the boys more than they can learn effectively, it will merely destroy that crisp timing that makes a team click. Hustle, confidence, good physical condition, and soundly taught fundamentals will blend into the will to win if the coach gives his boys an opportunity to fight for something worthwhile—to fight for a victory over capable opponents, which should be the goal of every athlete.

We here at the University of Kentucky spend part of every afternoon working on fundamentals. It may please the reader to know that during our 1947-48 campaign, after we had come through the hardest schedule ever faced by a college team in America, we went to New York and fought our way to the finals of the Olympic try-outs with the Phillips 66 team of Bartlesville, Oklahoma (National A.A.U. Champions for six consecutive times). To give you an idea as to how we feel about our fundamentals, the day before our game with Phillips we worked out for an hour in Madison Square Garden. The first thirty minutes were spent in spot or position shooting. Our fundamental drills had been so well mastered that I could call on our captain, give him the names and numbers of the drills, and tell him how often I wanted them run; the sequence of the drills had already been established.

After our thirty-minute shooting period, I walked over to Captain Kenneth Rollins and said, "I want you to go through all of our fundamental offensive drills twice and add to these our series of plays." Rollins called the team together and said, "Let's go on our fundamentals." Every boy on the squad knew what to do and immediately took his correct position. For the next fifteen minutes they ran through those drills with a lot of snap and a great deal of enthusiasm. Here was a bunch of boys who had already been in New York for about nine days, most of them ready to go home. They had played through a hard and difficult schedule but they still had a lot of eagerness for the drills. They knew that these drills had made them the clever basketball players that they were, resulting in several of them achieving All-American selections in 1947 and every one of them being placed on the All-Southeastern Conference team.

I stood at the end of the floor and watched the boys. I did not notice that Alvin Julian of Holy Cross and several of his players were seated across the floor because a number of spectators were present. After the drills, Coach Julian came over to me and said, "That was the finest exhibition of ball handling that I have ever seen. My boys thought your team was terrific. It is easy to see why Kentucky is a great team. Your kids were flawless. They certainly know what to do."

As the day wore on his words began to mean more and more to me, and I remember them now as one of the finest compliments that has ever been paid to my team.

4

Passing

The most important fundamental is that of passing the ball. We spend hours of hard work on passing. To the average individual, this may sound absurd. The first thing that I look for on an opposing team is how they "handle" the ball. This is the key that tells whether they are a high-class club or not. If they have smart and crafty passers who can size up the situations, who know when to pass and when to withhold the ball from play, who can pass true and with deception, then you can depend on an interesting evening, for the baskets will surely follow.

Accurate and well timed passing is the key to successful play. A team of indifferent passers may show up well in goal shooting in practice. The same team will make a sorry showing in a game, while a team that excels in the art of passing—although often making an indifferent showing in goal shooting while in practice—will often shine brilliantly under fire.

In passing a ball to a teammate not in motion, or one coming straight in, the pass should be made to a point in the region of the hips. If passed to the head, or even as high as the shoulders, it may cause fumbling because the ball must be adjusted before it can be passed again. Hard passes can be handled best if passed in the region near the waist. In passing to a player moving diagonally across the floor, the pass can be made higher, but never above the shoulders. It takes skill, gained only by hard practice, to be able to pass accurately to a running player at different distances and different rates of speed, so that the ball will reach the player at the proper point for easy and quick handling. Spend a lot of the daily practice on passing. Teach the players to use the push pass, the underhand pass, the hook pass, and the bounce pass. Tall men should make excellent use of the hook pass, especially when closely guarded.

If a player is having difficulty in getting the passes, the chances are that he is not going to meet the pass or that he is taking his eyes off the ball before it reaches him.

A team should have a good sense of appreciation for ball possession and take pride in it. A team is not in danger if it has possession of the ball and knows what to do with it. A team that has good passing will retain possession of the ball.

Timing is an essential element in accurate passing. It is, therefore, necessary to be able to judge the speed of the players and determine how hard the passes should be thrown to them. Passes should be fast, but not necessarily hard. Judgment in passing can only be gained by experience against good competition. It is not necessary in our style of play for a player to be a master of all types of passing, but he must be able to execute the passes accurately from the position that has been assigned to him.

A player should use deception in passing. In other words, faking plays an important part in passing and will often release an offensive man, especially against a man-to-man defense in which players will take risks to intercept passes.

In all of our passing, we attempt to get the ball to our receivers in the outside area away from the defensive man.

Catching the ball

In catching the ball, I think it is well to discuss the fundamental position of a basketball player. A player should have the weight on his toes or on the ball of his foot. His knees should be bent, his hips should be down, his back straight, and his head up. His hands should be advanced, the elbows in, and he should go to meet the pass. If at an angle, he should always go to meet the pass and then straighten out in the direction that he wishes to go. He should keep his eye on the ball. His hands should be in funnel-shape. The fingers should be spread and the ball should be met first with the finger tips and then the force of the ball should be allowed to come on the palm of the hand. The hands should give slightly on impact of the ball and the arms should carry immediately into position for a shot or a pass. In catching a low pass, the little fingers will be pointing toward each other and the thumbs will be out. In catching a high pass, the thumbs will be in.

Two-handed chest pass

This is the most commonly used pass in basketball and can be employed from any position on the floor. It is usually used for distances up to twenty feet in length. The pass is executed by having the body bent forward from the waist and by holding the ball directly in front of the body, chest high, the fingers covering the side of the ball with the thumbs behind the ball pointing inward. The elbows should be in close to the body and the ball should be released with a push and a snap of the wrist and the fingers. A good arm follow-through should complete the pass.

Two-handed bounce pass

This pass is executed in about the same manner as the two-handed chest pass with the exception of the fact that the ball strikes the floor and bounces into the hands of the receiver.

The body should be in a well balanced and crouched position, the arms extending upward, and the ball released with a wrist and finger snap so that the palms of the hands will be facing the floor, thumbs in. It is not necessary to put a spin on the ball as the natural force of the ball hitting the floor will give it the proper bounce. The ball should strike the floor in a region near the feet of the defensive player.

This pass is used: (1) to pass under a defensive man where it is excellent in penetrating the first line of a zone defense; (2) to get the ball in to the pivot man when the opposing center is playing aggressively on the pivot man; (3) on out-of-bounds plays. This pass is ordinarily not a long one, and is most advantageous in fast play near the basket. It should always be made on the outside away from the defensive man and should be received in the area between the outside knee and the hip.

Two-handed underhand pass

This pass is best used in a short-pass and pivot game and permits fast handling of the ball. It is usually handled on a lower plane than the other varieties of passes.

The player should be in a crouched position and the pass is ordinarily made by grasping the ball on the sides with the fingers well spread, thumbs pointing down and slightly inward. Draw the ball back near the right or the left hip with the opposite foot forward. If passing from the right side, the right arm will be bent and almost parallel to the body, while the left arm will be at right angles to the other arm. The pass is released with a snap of the wrist, the arms extended. Upon completion of the pass, the thumbs will be pointing upward and out. (See Plates 1 and 2.)

One-handed underhand pass

We use this pass a lot here at the University of Kentucky because we think it gives excellent protection for the ball in passing. It is also used extensively by those teams employing the figure-eight offense or by teams when stalling the ball. It is also utilized in a short-pass and pivot game.

The player is crouched in a position similar to that of a bowler. The elbows are bent and close to the side of the body. The wrist is bent downward and the hand is behind the ball with the thumb pointing outward. The arm is drawn back and when extended with an upward, full movement, the palm of the hand should face upward and the fingers should point towards the receiver. The ball is released with a wrist snap and the arm follows through. (See Plates 3, 4, and 5.)

For passing with the right hand, the left hand will be used to help adjust the ball.

Our forwards use this pass particularly in passing to the pivot man, and frequently our pivot man uses it from a crouched position in passing to cutters at the basket.

Two-handed overhead pass

This pass is generally used by tall players or by a receiver who, having caught a high pass, wishes to make a quick return pass. It is made by carrying the ball upward to a position above the head, both arms extended, the hands covering the sides and rear of the ball, the thumbs behind, and the elbows slightly bent. It is executed by stepping forward with either foot and throwing the ball with a forward and slightly downward motion of the arms. (See Plates 6 and 7.)

One-handed overhead pass

This is sometimes referred to as the baseball pass and may be used from any position on the floor. It is employed by the guards to get a ball away quickly from the defensive basket. It is generally a long and a hard pass.

If the pass is thrown with the right hand, the ball is brought back in an area just back of the right ear. The right hand will be behind the ball. The left hand, again, will be used to help adjust the ball to the throwing position. As the ball is brought to the throwing position the weight will be shifted to the right foot in the rear. As the ball is thrown, the weight will be shifted to the left foot as the entire body is put into the throw. When the pass is completed the position of the player will be very much like that of a man who has thrown a baseball. (See Plates 8, 9, 10, and 11.)

Right and left shoulder pass

The ball is held by both hands with the fingers pointing upward, the thumbs behind and below the ball pointing inward. The elbows should be flexed. The shoulders and upper arms do little in the execution of this pass as it is made by the full extension of the arms from the elbows and a wrist snap. The ball is held near the body, the shoulders high.

The advantage of this pass is that it enables the passer to keep the ball away from a defensive player by placing his entire body between the defensive man and the ball. It is used near the sidelines and beneath the basket.

Hook pass

The hook pass is best used by tall men, and when defensive men play close. It serves its purpose most effectively for long distances and is used by teams employing the fast break offense. Guards use it successfully in getting the ball away from the defensive basket. It is a difficult pass to guard against.

The ball is held in the throwing hand, waist high, fingers spread, the ball against the wrist. The ball is held in the right hand, and the left hand is turned to the defensive man. The player takes one step away, jumps, turns in the air, looks, passes, and alights facing the opponent, knees bent, hips down, ready to swing into play.

Slap pass or shove pass

This pass merely deflects the ball without catching it. It may be made with one hand or with both hands. It is most effective in close-in play where a fast return must be made or on held balls where it may not be possible to obtain possession of the ball.

Flip pass

This pass is used for close passing and in pivoting offense. The wrist is used to flip the ball to a player cutting by. It is a short pass, generally from two to five feet in length. It is used primarily in the "give and go" offense and is seldom intercepted or fumbled due to the fact that the ball is protected and shielded from the defensive man.

The pass is made almost entirely with a wrist flip and we employ it extensively in giving a return pass to our guards who are cutting by toward the basket. Our pivot men use it to feed guards and forwards who have been freed by our screening offense.

One-handed roll pass

This pass is not used extensively, but it does have definite advantages. It is used to pass by a defense man who has assumed a fairly definite stance, and is also used to pass the ball in from out of bounds as it has a surprise element. It is used to get the ball in to a pivot man.

The pass is made very much like the one-handed underhand pass, although in this case the player is in a more crouched position. It is sometimes best made by dropping the body in such a position that one knee is almost on the floor. The hand is brought back and the ball is thrown forward with a slight wrist snap and arm follow through. The palm of the hand will face the individual receiving the pass. The ball is rolled on the floor to a teammate. (See Plates 12, 13, and 14.)

The backhand pass

This is also a pass that is not used a great deal, but it has tremendous possibilities when it is used properly. Some boys greatly abuse this pass by thinking it is a fancy one, but that is certainly not the use for it. It is used a lot by the Eastern teams in their "give and go" game. It is used extensively where a dribbler cuts into the basket and is cut off from in front, so that he cannot make a shot or pass, so he flips it around behind his body to a teammate who is either open or who is cutting for the basket.

There are various ways of throwing this ball. The pivot man sometimes uses the backhand pass to flip the ball around behind him to feed men who are cutting for the basket. The way the pass is executed will depend entirely upon the situation. This pass when used by a dribbler who has been cut off going into the basket is made by carrying the hand opposite the defensive man down, the ball cupped with the hand and wrist, and by means of a backhand motion of the arm and a wrist flip the ball is thrown behind the back with the palm of the hand finishing facing the individual who is receiving the pass. (See Plates 15, 16, 17, and 18.)

Fumbling (causes)

1. Hard pass.
2. Misjudged speed.

3. Inaccurate pass—too high or too low.
4. Fatigue.
5. Fighting ball.
6. Not keeping cool.
7. Weak fingers and wrists. (Remedy: press small rubber ball.)

Passing hints

1. The first fundamental to learn is that of handling the ball.
2. In receiving a pass, go to meet it. It may be at an angle. Catch the ball, then straighten out.
3. Do not pass to a man going away from you.
4. Pass across the floor. The pass is less apt to be intercepted.
5. Time your passes. Don't throw wild.
6. Pass to the region of the waistline. The passes are more easily handled. You then can dribble, pass, pivot, or shoot without adjusting the ball.
7. Pass to a position where a teammate can get it.
8. Do not telegraph passes.
9. Learn to receive and pass in one motion.
10. Throw quickly and accurately, not too hard.
11. In one-handed passes, the foot opposite the throwing arm should go forward with the throw.
12. Pass only to the man in position to receive the pass.
13. Release potential receivers with a deceptive move before throwing to them.
14. Do not pass laterally under your own basket. Pass *out*.
15. To a man in motion, give a lead suitable to his speed.

5

Shooting

Knowing when *not* to shoot is just as important as knowing when to shoot. I would say that, taking an average situation, a player should shoot only when there is a reasonable chance of making a goal. Just to take a chance shot with little hope of making it is merely inviting the opponents to take the ball. A player should never shoot when off balance, or when the shot is exceedingly long, or when his teammates are not in an excellent position to follow the shot and recover the ball in case he misses. This is true in every case except in the dying seconds of a game when such a hope shot might accidentally connect and bring victory.

Possibly the most important fundamental in the training of a basketball team is in goal shooting, for the winning of a game depends on this. Goal shooting is to basketball what putting is to golf.

Good goal shooting requires constant practice in order to bring about perfect judgment of distance.

Some coaches say that basketball players are born, not made. If this were a fact, then coaching would certainly be a simple occupation. It is true that some boys have more natural ability than others, but I feel that it is a reflection on our profession if we brush the statement off this lightly. Good goal shots can be developed. They need not necessarily be born that way. The secret of good goal shooting is constant practice in doing all phases correctly and, therefore, forming a habit. Some boys are not good goal shooters because there is a flaw in the mechanical technique that they employ. A coach can help a boy form correct habits and break the bad habits he may have. Goal shooting has increased percentagewise in the last ten years. Ten years ago a 30 per cent shooting average would win most games. The one-handed shot was not too prevalent. But today you will find dozens of variations of one-handed shots.

Many of the freshmen who come to the university have established fabulous records in high school. After they are here we find that they are not such good goal shots as we thought. The boys will come to us and say, "I can't hit so well as I did in high school." The reason for this is not that the boy is a poor shot; it is merely that the defense against his shot is so much better. In high school, very often, a boy will find very poor defensive men playing against him. But in college scouts will soon report the habits of this boy and a defensive man will be assigned to stop him.

According to recent figures, we have many boys that hit some 40 to 60 per cent of all the shots that they attempt. In fact, according to the figures released by the NCAB on April 8, 1956, thirty-two college players shot with an average of .478 upward to .647 for the entire preceding season. This was unheard of years ago and is entirely the result of jump shooting and one-handed shooting, which has become the standard today.

I feel that most of the goal shooting done by players in practice is absolutely wrong. In watching teams warm up, I notice that they always form into a semicircle about twenty feet from the basket and everyone starts shooting from there. They usually spend the entire goal-shooting period out there. Let me ask you a question—

how many of your players score goals in a game from those positions? Why not practice shots from the positions in which your players will attempt them in competition? If you will carefully check a number of games, you will see that the least guarded of any spot on the floor is the area within twelve feet of the basket, and you will also notice that the greatest percentage of shots missed are missed in this area. The reason for this is that you seldom see boys practicing their shots at this distance.

We, here at Kentucky, practice our goal shooting to conform to our plays—to the actual place where we get opportunities in a game. We never allow our forwards or guards to practice goal shooting from any other position than those from which they have opportunities in a game.

Our left forward will always shoot on his side of the floor because the only opportunities he will get will be from the positions that have been assigned to him. His rebounding will be from that side of the floor also, and we feel that it is useless for him to practice shooting from every position on the floor if he does not get an opportunity to do so in a game. We feel that if a boy specializes on his position, we can improve our goal shooting tremendously.

We also have a theory here at Kentucky that the fundamental shot in basketball is the long shot. Coaches frequently say, "Kentucky is lucky because they always have good long shots." That may be true but we wish also to take a little credit for this because we spend hours in faithful work in practicing these long shots. We feel this way about it: If you can hit long shots you can always get the close-in shots because the defense must come out to cover the shooters. If you can not hit long, the defense will float and concentrate near the basket, and your players will not be permitted to crash in for close-in shots. That is the reason why we specialize on position, or spot, shooting and on long shooting.

There is some question in the minds of coaches as to whether the backboard should be used in shooting. We feel that all long shots should eliminate the use of the backboard and that all dribble-in shots should make use of the backboard. There is an area on each side of the backboard where it may be advisable to bank a shot. We make it a fast rule that all lay-up shots must make use of the backboard, and when a dribbler comes in directly in front of the board, we require him to go to the side and bank the shot. We have found from actual experience and from hours of practice with lay-up shots attempted from in front of the basket where the backboard is not used, that invariably a goodly number of them hit the back of the ring and bounce out. This can be eliminated entirely by merely cutting a foot or so to the side and banking the shot.

Spot shooting

We believe in specialized spot shooting. We believe that our players should not practice all over the floor, but should learn to shoot from certain designated areas; in our system of play they will get shots from those areas and usually only from those. We drill our men to shoot from certain positions, as our plays have taught us that they will get shots from those areas in a game. A man may never get a shot from a certain position on the floor and there is no use for him to practice from all the positions. Again, we have devised our fundamental shooting drills according to the use we have for them.

In the following diagrams, I have illustrated the places where we get our shots and where we practice our shots. Whenever we get in these positions, we feel that we have a thirty-three per cent chance of making a successful shot and, therefore, we take it.

The forward on the left-hand side of the court facing the basket will shoot from the position indicated (Chart 1). He will reverse

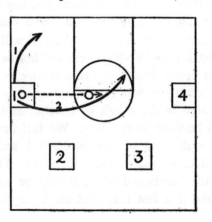

Chart 1.

and go in as shown by line number 1. Or he may receive a pass and cut in front of the pivot man and shoot anywhere along the line number 2. As another alternative, he will pass to the pivot man and receive a pass back from him.

Our guards in their shooting must be more versatile than the forwards. They will get shots from almost anywhere on the floor, but most of them will come from the four positions that I have numbered 1, 2, 3, and 4. In positions 1 and 4 they will shoot over the screener (Chart 1). They will go in on guard-around plays (Chart 2) or they will screen for each other and go in as indicated (Chart 3). The forward in position 1 (Chart 1) during the course

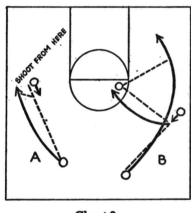

Chart 2.

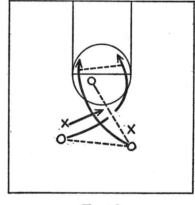

Chart 3.

of the year will never shoot from the right-hand side of the floor. The forward number 4 will shoot from his position, reverse and go in to the basket, dribble in front of the pivot man or pass to the pivot man, and cut off of him, or screen for the guard and allow the guard to shoot over him.

In our shooting drills we play for percentage shots from these specialized positions. We believe, as we have said before, that the fundamental shot in basketball is the long shot and not the short shot. We believe that if you can hit from the positions indicated on the diagrams, the opponent cannot afford to play a sinking defensive game against you but must come out and play you strongly, man to man. If they do that, then you can set up your screening plays and run them effectively. Failure to be able to hit long shots will cause the defense to concentrate around the basket and you will never be able to get in for your close shots. Therefore, the fundamental shot in basketball is the long shot.

Two-handed push shot

The two-handed push shot can be employed from almost any position on the floor. It is the oldest of our shots. Up until 1930 almost every shot taken from the floor was a two-handed push shot. One-handed shots, until that time, were regarded as frills or "show-off" shots. We believed for a long time that the two-handed push shot was the most accurate and soundest shot that we could employ. Up until 1948 on our national championship team every boy could shoot this shot. After seeing this team play, one sportswriter described it as "a good, sound, fundamental team that still uses the two-handed shots."

By 1951 our national championship team of that year was using many varieties of the one-handed shot; but all of our "out-on-the-floor" shots were two-handed shots. Our guards always used them when shooting from a distance, and our forwards did likewise. However, in close to the basket they were all using one-handed shots. Our undefeated national championship team of 1953 was a modern team in all respects. Fully four-fifths of the shots taken by this team were variations of the one-handed shots, and only those shots taken from out 25 feet or more were two-handed shots. I would say that the same condition has prevailed in the past year. We still use the two-handed push shot when shooting 25 feet or more from the basket.

There are two theories as to the stance that should be employed in making this shot. One group, largely in the East, likes to keep both feet together or slightly spread, but on the same line. We like to use a stance in which the left foot is slightly ahead of the right foot because we believe that it gives a more natural, more flexible, and more comfortable position.

We like to crouch with the knees bent, the hips down, head up; and from this position without changing the position of the feet, we can shoot, dribble, pass, or pivot. We feel that such a position has the advantage over the position in which both feet are together on the same line.

The ball should be held with the elbows in close to the body, directly in front of the body, chest high. The ball should be held by the fingertips and not against the heels of the hands. We like to bring the ball downward to the waistline in order to relax the muscles, then bring it up along the abdomen and chest and release it with a snap when it reaches a height above the eyes. The hands should be rotated so that the finish of the shot leaves the thumbs close together and the palms directed toward the basket. The index finger will be the last to leave the ball. It is not necessary to put extra spin on the ball as the shot will give it the proper amount of "english." (See Plate 19.)

We have always maintained that a player should concentrate in his shooting. In other words, do not just throw the ball at the basket; look at the basket, get it fixed in your mind and keep it as an objective until after the shot has been made and a complete follow-through has been finished. Then, look for the ball and get into position for the rebound. The arch of the shot should be fairly high but not exaggerated. Even if the shot misses and should hit the backboard above the goal, a good arch may still result in a basket. A shot with a good arch is always easier to rebound. If the shot has been properly executed, it will be a soft shot that will rebound naturally.

Get uniformity into your shooting. On long shots, hurry to get in fairly close with both feet together so that you can move in either direction for the rebound.

Two-handed underhand shot

Probably the first shot ever taken at a basket by anyone will be the two-handed underhand shot. In watching a group of small boys play, I observed that every one of them used it. It seemed to them to be a way of lifting the ball into the basket. Since this shot is so easily made it becomes the most mechanical of all of our shots. Some call it the free-throw shot although it can be used from any part of the floor. One handicap to its use as a scoring threat from the floor is the fact that it is started so low and the hands finish so much lower than in our other shots, that it is easier to block.

All of the boys on our 1948 National Championship team, with the exception of one, used this shot at the free-throw line. Our average for the season on free-throws was 62.5, which is not considered bad when you take into consideration the fact that we competed in one of the most difficult schedules and series of post-season tournament games, finishing with the Phillips 66 Oilers in the finals of the Olympic Try-Outs in Madison Square Garden.

Since the foul rule has been changed to give a bonus free-throw if the first free-throw is made, we have felt that more premium should be placed on free-throwing. Formerly, we permitted our boys to go to the free-throw line and take any type of shot that they felt they could make. Our free-throwing stayed in the 62 per cent range. However, we noticed that some of the best teams we watched play required all of their boys to take the two-handed underhand shot at the free-throw line. We have always believed that this was the most accurate shot to use in that situation. And so, during the 1953–54 and 1954–55 seasons, we required everybody to shoot free-throws in this fashion. We got some improvement, but not so much as we had hoped. Then, in the 1955–56 season, we made it a rule that anyone with an average of 60 per cent or better could shoot one-handed. Otherwise he would have to go back to the two-handed underhand shot. We finally managed to get the following averages: Bob Burrow, *two-handed*, 66.2 per cent; Jerry Bird, *one-handed*, 67.3 per cent; Vernon Hatton, *two-handed*, 67.6 per cent; Gerry Calvert, *two-handed*, 64.1 per cent; Phil Grawemeyer, *one-handed*, 73.3 per cent; while Bill Cassady, shooting *one-handed*, had an average of 95.2 per cent. The Kentucky team shot an average of 65.6 per cent while our opponents were shooting 66.5 per cent.

It is interesting to note that in the state high school tournament played in Lexington during March of 1956 there were 880 free-throw attempts made by the high school boys; and they were successful in 67 per cent of them. When you consider that these lads averaged in age from fourteen to eighteen years, while our college boys averaged from nineteen to twenty-three years, it is apparent that our free-throwing should be improved. Although we devote as much as thirty minutes a day to free-throwing, we are not getting the results that we should like.

It is difficult to say which shot should be used at the free-throw line, but the following statistics can be presented with accuracy.

In the 1955–56 season fifty members of major college teams were successful in 77.8 per cent of their attempts from the free-throw line, with twenty-six of them above 80.1 per cent. It is also interesting to note that there were thirty major college teams that had an average better than 69.5 per cent, with twenty-three of them shooting better than 70 per cent of their shots. These figures are merely given as a guide when shooting techniques are discussed.

The stance at the free-throw line again varies. Some coaches prefer that both feet should be placed evenly on the line about twelve inches apart. However, we believe, again, that a more comfortable position can be assured when the left foot is placed immediately back of the line and the right foot is placed eight or ten inches back of it. We believe that the body bends more naturally in this fundamental position for it allows the player to be on his toes, his knees bent, his hips down, his back straight, and his head up. I cannot emphasize this too much because I think it is all-important. It is the natural way and the easy way to shoot the underhand shot.

In free-throwing, a boy may be tense when he comes to the free-throw line because it may be a critical situation in the game and it is always important to make a free throw—it always takes two points to beat it. To relieve this tenseness, our boys bounce the ball on the floor as often as four times and we tell them not to look at the basket until they are ready to make the shot. This usually brings complete relaxation.

Place the fingers on the sides of the ball and keep the palm of the hand off the ball. The fingers should be spread pointing slightly downward, while the thumbs should be pointed forward. The ball should be held with both hands at waist level. In executing the shot, the knees will bend to a comfortable position, the arms will bend but will be close to the sides of the body. The ball will be raised forward and upward with full extension of the arms. It is preferred by some coaches that a small amount of wrist snap be given but this is not necessary. No spin need be given to the shot as a small amount of rotation will be given the ball as the shot is executed. It is believed by some that the shooter, in starting the shot, should take a full, deep breath. We feel that this is helpful. Be sure that there is a complete follow-through on this shot. Sometimes the weight

will be shifted to the front foot so much that the shooter will take
a step after the shot leaves his hands in order to get in a good follow-
up position. This may be exaggerated, but the point is this: Do not
pull the shot by causing the hands to come up too high with the
result that the ball falls short of its mark. Try for uniformity on
these throws to the point where the motions become mechanical.
(See Plates 20, 21, and 22.)

Free-throwing is all-important; games are won and lost at the
free-throw line. Some coaches require that all players throw fifty
free-throws per day. We like to finish with a fifteen-minute free-
throw shooting period after practice and we believe that the boys
will be more deliberate and take more time where the time element
is involved than they will when a specific number of throws are
required.

Two-handed overhead shot

This shot is usually employed by tall men to shoot over shorter
men. It is used after a rebound has been taken, or after a high pass
has been received. The shot is generally of a medium distance as
the shooter quickly loses accuracy as he moves away from the
basket.

In executing the shot, the ball is held directly above the head,
the elbows are slightly bent, the thumbs are below and to the rear
of the ball, the knees are slightly bent, the head up, facing the
basket. As the ball is released the arms are extended and the body
moves slightly forward on the toes as the knees straighten. (See
Plates 23, 24, and 25.)

One-handed shots

It is difficult to discuss the one-handed shot because there are
so many variations of it. It has been a development of the past
fifteen years, with the greatest concentration having been focused
on it during the past ten years. There is a definite use for the one-
handed shot and it will always be a part of the game, although many
coaches fifteen years ago strongly restrained their teams in its use.
Shooting has become so accurate and so pronounced, and scoring
has become so important, in the past few years that individual
and team marks today seem fantastic.

In the season just closed there were eighty-six players on major college teams who scored 19 points or more per game; and there were thirty-two players who were so accurate in shooting from the field that they scored with an average of from 47.8 per cent to a sensational 64.7 per cent. There were fifty teams that scored from an average of from 78.6 to 95.9 points per game for the entire season. The shooting percentages of the teams were just as sensational, since twenty-eight major college teams shot 41 per cent for the entire season. Again these figures are given only as a guide to emphasize the tremendous scoring potential of individuals and teams in recent years.

There are several types of one-handed shots and it is best to discuss them as to their most effective usefulness.

One-handed dribble-in shot

This is sometimes referred to as the "crip" or the "lay-up" shot. It is made by a dribbler dribbling in to the basket, taking off on the opposite foot from the hand with which he is shooting, using a high jump and a full extension of the arm to place the ball against the board and banking it in.

In coming in from the right side, the right hand would be used and from the left side, the left hand would be used. It merely gives the shooter additional protection by placing his body between the ball and the defensive man so that a slight bump will not cause the shot to fail. As the shooting arm goes up above the head, the ball is slightly pushed when it leaves the hand. Some players prefer to place the hand behind the ball, while others prefer to lay the ball on the fingertips and roll it off into the basket.

In dribbling in, a shooter should keep his eye on the basket using a high jump, not a broad jump, and should not put a spin on the ball; a perfectly dead ball will be the most accurate. In using a dribble-in shot directly in front of the basket, it is well to go to either side and place the ball against the board rather than attempt to throw it in dead directly from the front.

One-handed, under the basket shot (right or left)

This shot is used when a player has taken the ball off the backboard, or when he receives a pass while standing under or cutting under the basket. To execute a right-handed shot after taking a rebound while facing the basket, step out sideways to the right from under the basket with the left foot crossing in front of the right foot. Shift the weight over the left foot and take off with that foot, pivoting upon it as foot and body turn toward the basket. Rise in the air turning toward the basket. Straighten the right arm fully and, with a wrist snap, lay the ball against the backboard, fingers behind the ball. The shot may be made with the left hand provided the right foot is used as a take-off.

One-handed turn around shot (right or left)

This shot is made when a player receives a pass near the basket with his back toward the basket. Many of our pivot men today prefer to jockey their defensive man into such a position that the defensive man plays behind them and gives them a position shot.

As the ball is caught with both hands, the shooter may use a fake with his head, his shoulders, the ball, or in any way mislead his opponent as to his real intent. If the shooter wishes to shoot with his right hand he will step to the left with his left foot. As the movement begins, the ball will be brought over to the left side of the body with both hands, the left hand being used more or less as a guide. When the push-off is made with the left foot, the body will turn and face the basket as the right arm is raised and straightened out and the ball released with the maximum upward extension. The fingers will be behind the ball. As the shooter comes down he will alight with knees bent, facing the basket, ready to rebound the shot. The shooter should look for the basket as soon as he starts the shot as it is highly important to have a good view of the basket in order to insure accuracy. It is well to use the backboard for this shot unless the shooter is directly in front of the basket. (See Plates 26, 27, 28, 29, 30, and 31.)

In executing the shot with the left hand, change the shooting hand and take-off foot, just the opposite from that of the right-handed shot.

One hand, in motion push shot

This shot is used following a straight or diagonal drive for the basket. The position of the hands on the ball after the last dribble, the moving of the ball into the shooting position, and the take-off, are the same as for the lay-up shot.

For a right-hand shot, take off on the left foot, transferring the ball into the shooting hand, resting it on the fingertips. Extend the shooting arm forward and upward. The ball should be released with a finger push at the height of the jump, arms fairly well extended. The body should land slightly bent, knees flexed, with the weight on the forward right foot ready to follow.

Set position shot

There are two variations of this shot:

(1) Western Style: In shooting with the right hand, the right foot is forward, knees bent, hips down, the ball resting on the left hand, the right hand behind the ball, both thumbs pointing to the left. The shot is executed by a slight knee bend, the push being given by the right hand behind the ball. It may be made with a slight jump, or it may be made with both feet remaining on the floor, the weight on the toes (See Plates 32, 33, and 34.)

(2) The Step-in: This shot is more commonly used in the Middle West and the South. It is executed, if thrown with the right hand, by stepping with the left foot and using it as a take-off. The execution is the same as in the Western style although the ball is held higher.

Cross-arm shot, or right or left shoulder shot

This shot is best used when the guard forces the shooter away from the basket or when the shooter is closely guarded near the basket.

The ball is lifted into shooting position with both hands above the shoulders, the elbows bent, placing the ball away from the opponent. The ball is thrown upward from the shoulder and diagonally across the face by the straightening of the elbows.

Flip shot

This shot is executed especially by the pivot man with his back toward the basket. As the ball is caught with both hands it is held in front, the knees bent and the weight evenly distributed on both feet. If the shot is attempted with the right hand, as the jump is made the body turns to the right, the ball is held above the head with the right hand. At the height of the jump the arm is fully extended and as the ball is released it is given a slight flip with the wrist. The hand will face the basket. This is also called the "jump turn around shot." (See Plates 35, 36, 37, and 38.)

Very few men have the patience to practice this shot although Aggie Sale, our two-times All American, and George Yates, our All Southern center, were deadly with this shot.

Tip shot

This may not be legitimately called a shot, but since it is an attempt at a field goal, it must be so classified. It is a shot attempted by tall men who can effectively rebound.

The ball should be tipped with widespread fingers and should be tapped at the height of the take-off. The shot is tried when the ball is free under the offensive basket.

Bob Burrow, our All-American center in 1956, was a very outstanding tip-shot man. His timing was excellent. His ability to sense where the ball would come off of the board was outstanding, and with his excellent timing he tipped in as many as 7 goals after other players had missed in the attempt. We always classified these as cheap baskets.

There are other mechanical pet shots that are used by players, but we do not believe it worthwhile to discuss these. There are many freak shots that are effective, but for general, all-around, sound basketball, the above-mentioned shots will prove satisfactory.

Shooting hints

1. Relax.
2. Be deliberate.
3. Have comfortable body balance.
4. Do not take hope shots. Be sensible.
5. Gauge the distance.
6. Shoot for the basket.
7. Locate the basket; concentrate; look.
8. Watch the ball until it hits or misses.
9. Have reasonable arch that can be rebounded.

10. Follow all of your shots.
11. Practice at top speed.
12. Practice the shots that you will get in a game.
13. Practice close in, then move out.
14. Study the backboard. (Glass is faster than wood.)
15. Get muscular coordination.
16. Shoot when you are "on"; pass to teammates when you are "off."
17. Be unselfish. There is enough glory in victory for everyone.

6

Dribbling

Too many of our ball clubs today employ entirely too much useless dribbling. The proper use of the dribble may add a tremendous threat to a ball club's reputation but, in far too many situations, it will prove more harmful than beneficial. Dribbling is spectacular from a spectator's standpoint and a great many players use it as a method of focusing attention on themselves during the game.

Dribbling may be used as an offensive and a defensive threat. There are several situations where the dribble can be used to advantage in every game. The most common of these is in taking the ball away from the defensive basket before the man with the ball can be tied up by the opponents. Ordinarily, only one or two dribbles are necessary to get away from this danger area and then the ball should be passed to a teammate as quickly as possible.

Dribbling may be used in advancing the ball to the defense and also to draw defensive men away from the basket. It is used in short drives toward the basket especially on guard-around plays, or where the ball has been given by the pivot man to someone cutting by. In addition the dribble is employed on the fast break to advance the ball, particularly when the other players are behind the man with the ball.

A short dribble is often useful in getting the ball away at the center jump, and on held ball situations. It is also an important weapon in allowing a man to escape from a pressing defensive situation, and following an intercepted pass it may make it possible to move quickly into offensive territory and possibly score. When all the other men are covered, it may be used by the dribbler to gain a new position which will enable him to pass the ball to a teammate.

These are all specific situations where the dribble will prove useful, but for a player to merely dribble the ball with no exact purpose in mind has never been satisfactory. A good rule to follow is: Never dribble the ball when it is possible to pass.

Dribbling technique

In order to dribble correctly, the dribbler should stay on his toes, his knees should be bent, his body crouched. His head should be up and his arm almost fully extended. The ball will be bounced. The player's elbow will be low and the forearm almost parallel to the floor. In dribbling, the fingers will be cupped and well spread and the ball will be bounced with a wrist motion, the elbows rising and falling but very little. The ball will be pushed and not batted.

In early drilling on this maneuver, it may be best not to try for speed, but after the execution has been well mastered, it will be wise to travel at top speed since the dribble is designed to cover distance.

The height that the ball will bounce varies. In an ordinary dribble the ball will bounce possibly two feet, but where extreme speed is necessary, a higher and longer dribble will be used. Some players, in executing our plays, are able to get into position with but one dribble while others need two or more. This is merely a difference in the speed of the dribbler.

In our guard-around play and in virtually all of our offensive guard movements that are described in Chapter 14, "Offensive Guard Play," it will be seen that we take only one dribble before we shoot. When more than one dribble is necessary we find that the timing is entirely too slow.

Some dribblers prefer to keep the ball in front of them. We believe that the ball is usually directly in front of the right or left arm, depending on which one is being used for the dribble. Body protection should be given to the ball and the ball should be kept to the side away from the defensive man. The dribbler should always be in position so that he can stop, pivot, turn, shoot, or pass. When he stops he should be in a crouched position over the ball and not upright. This will give the necessary protection to the ball and will prevent the dribbler from moving his pivot foot.

Objections to the dribble

It has been mentioned before that one of the chief objections to the dribble is that it causes selfishness. Four of the teammates remain idle while the dribbler is maneuvering the ball. This, of course, is desirable if the maneuver is designed to set up a scoring play but if it causes indecision in the minds of the teammates it would be best to eliminate the move.

Another chief objection to the use of the dribble is that it permits the defense time to cover the other offensive players. A player who is not expert in the use of the dribble will often lose the other men on the floor and not know where or when it is best to pass the ball.

Cautions in the use of the dribble

The dribble should never be used if a pass can be made.

A dribble should not begin until the player is ready. Many players dribble as soon as they get the ball. Others have a habit of taking one bounce immediately after receiving a pass. This is a very bad habit and should be corrected immediately. Save the dribble for a threat. We tell our defensive men that as soon as a player has been forced to take up his dribble they should fly immediately at him and try to tie up the ball.

We found in one of our N.C.A.A. Tournament games that one of the players on the opposing team always took one dribble immediately after receiving a pass. Barker, a clever player with both hands, was assigned to guard this man and he stole several of the balls away from him because he knew exactly what the player would do as soon as he caught the pass. Barker was able to take the ball away from him twice for scores during the game due to the fact that this player was not in the habit of having an aggressive man guard him out in the front line.

7

Pivoting

Several years ago we were playing one of our traditional rivals and I heard two of my boys discussing one of the opposing players. The essence of the conversation was this: "He certainly is tough to guard because he can stop on a dime."

I asked the boys what they meant by that and soon we had a general discussion on this particular maneuver. It seemed that this player had the faculty of being able to dribble at top speed and then come to a stop, instantly, without cutting his stride or without the least preliminary slowing down. The next time that we played against this team, the subject was brought up again and it was found that this man was able to come to a dead stop better than anyone we had ever seen. He carried his body low and in stopping used a short jump with both of his feet striking the floor at the same time. The right foot was usually about eighteen inches ahead of the left. This was an excellent position from which the player could execute a turn or a pivot.

Our boys for several weeks after this practiced coming to a dead stop and I believe that we gained a great deal of valuable experience from this. In stopping, too many players slow down before coming to a stop and move their feet, shuffle, and finish in an unbalanced position. When a player is moving at terrific speed and a stop or a change of direction is necessary, he should be in such a position that his center of gravity is close to the floor. If a player comes to a stop by the use of steps, the movement is generally completed with a one-two count: that is, one foot finishes ahead of the other and is the last to hit the floor. Time is not wasted in teaching players how to stop properly. Too often a player in driving toward the basket, or in dribbling, will find that he must stop suddenly, and in doing so loses body balance and takes steps. This, naturally, loses the ball.

Turning and pivoting are usually considered as one and the same in basketball. It means reversing the position of a player. In other words, a player is cutting in one direction. He comes to a stop, turns and either faces back or cuts back in the opposite direction.

In the early twenties, the pivot was an essential part of every well executed offense. A player was taught how to dribble dead on to an opponent, stop, pivot, and face back, then cut by the opponent or to follow as a trailer to the man to whom he passed. This was known as a "short pass, pivoting, short shot" game. The zone defense and the shifting defense have played havoc with this type of offense because it is best used against a sticking man-to-man defense.

The pivot is also excellently employed against a charging defense and can be used to block out defensive players. Many coaches use it to free men on the inside screening attack.

Reverse pivot

In making a reverse pivot, stop with either foot forward. Most of the weight will be on the forward foot. As the turn is made on the balls of the feet, the weight will be shifted to the bent rear leg. In spinning, turn away from the side having the foot forward and take a full step to the rear with this forward foot. The weight will shift to the pivoting foot as the motion is completed.

Side-line pivot

It is one of the rules in basketball to always drive a dribbler to the sidelines. If this holds true, then a pivot must result. The defensive man will naturally be to the inside, therefore, to execute this pivot correctly, the inside foot should be forward and the weight should be on this foot. The turn should be made away from the defensive man or to the sideline. Consequently, the pivoter would face the sideline and turn on the balls of both feet. Then, take a step with the original forward foot directly to the rear, keeping the ball on the sideline side of the court, with the body bent, the ball away from the opponent. As the turn is completed, make a two-handed underhand pass, or better still, a one-handed underhand pass with the outside arm.

Front or roll pivot

The pivoter comes to a one-two stop with either the right or left foot forward, at such a distance from the defensive man that he has adequate ball protection. If the right foot is forward the weight is on that foot. In executing the pivot the left leg is swung in an arc to the rear and away from the right foot, the pivot being made on the ball of the right foot. As the left foot makes contact with the floor the weight is shifted to that foot. As the pivot is made the right shoulder is dropped and the back of the pivoter is turned to the defensive man. In other words, the pivoter rolls by his opponent and as the pivot foot (right) is raised, a two-handed or one-handed underhand pass is made.

Pivoting hints

1. Timing is essential in pivoting. The man working with the pivoter must do the timing. Do not come too soon. Come late and come fast.
2. Use pivoting to get away from the guard even if you haven't the ball.
3. Practice change-of-direction turns.
4. As a rule, pivot to the outside.
5. Threaten the guard, then step, reverse, and pass.

6. Feint pass but do not move feet; suck up the guard, then pivot by him.

7. In pivoting, pull away from the guard when passing to a trailer.

8. Keep low on all pivots. Be set to drive in any direction after the pivot is made.

9. After you pivot, you may run interference. Go the same way as the man to whom you passed. You will then be between the defensive man and the man to whom you passed, or you may give up the ball to the cutter, pivot and go in the opposite direction. By doing the latter you place the defensive man between yourself and your teammate. In this situation, if the defensive man follows the receiver, your teammate may give you a quick return pass.

8

Faking and Footwork

By faking we mean an action that is used to mislead an opponent and draw him out of a good position or off-balance. It is an intentional offensive or defensive move and can be made in many different ways depending on the situation. It can be made with the ball, the head, the shoulders, the arms, the eyes, the feet, the voice, or any combination of these. It is a maneuver that is contrary to the final intent of the user designed to make possible a planned operation. It is a move designed to gain an advantage for the user and can be a very important factor in team play.

The type of fake that is used will depend entirely on the situation and the ability of the man using it. The faking on the part of the pivot man has been described in the paragraph on pivot play. A foot fake, a head fake, a ball fake employed by a guard will very often mislead a defensive man and enable the guard to advance the ball to the forward. A fake on the part of the forward through the

58

use of his head and shoulder may draw a defensive man out so that the forward may reverse and go in to the basket.

A step in the opposite direction of that originally intended by the user may often lead a defensive player out of position and leave him flat-footed. A combination of faking movements may be used. A ball, head, and eye fake may be employed to draw an opponent on his toes to permit the player to dribble by. By faking a dribble with the ball and taking a step forward a player may be able to force a guard to retreat so that he can get a shot. A head and body fake to the right may draw an opponent to that side to enable a man to use a swinging, backward step with the left foot and a drive into the basket. The arms can be thrown up to make it appear that a player is about to receive a pass. This may draw an opponent up and enable the man to cut around him.

Our guards use fake passes into the forwards to draw up the defensive men and then permit the forwards to reverse and get a direct pass from the faker.

The eyes can be employed in many ways to deceive defensive men, especially in passes in from out-of-bounds plays. Our drill on fake passing is designed with this idea in mind: Be able to pass in the opposite direction from where you are looking. Our split vision drill teaches this.

You may fake an injury after a fall on the floor and then put on a burst of speed to temporarily catch a guard flat-footed.

Defensive men can also make use of the faking movements. When two offensive men approach one defensive man, he can fake a rushing movement at a dribbler to force him to stop and then fade back to cover the other player.

All of the movements that are used contrary to the final intent are faking movements and any combination of them can be employed.

Footwork

Another important fundamental is proper footwork. Under this subject we classify running, cutting, faking, dribbling, and every phase of play where the feet are involved. We have experimented with footwork so that our stance at any place on the floor is proper for a quick break from that particular position.

In lining up our forwards, we like to place them in our pivot post offense about one yard from the sideline. It is absolutely natural for a boy in lining up to place the leg nearest the defensive man ahead and have the sideline foot back. Some boys prefer to play this way and to use a sliding movement in going out to meet the pass. We prefer to have the court side foot ahead and the inside foot back, with the player facing with his body toward the center circle. In modern basketball, the guard will naturally play tight and parallel to the offensive man until that offensive man is out beyond the free-throw line. If this is true, and we have found it so, then we feel that in going out to meet the ball the first step should be taken with the inside foot, the ball being passed in the region of the outside hip, or with the bounce pass above the outside knee. If this footwork is used, it will instantly place the body of the offensive man between the ball and the defensive man, which is exactly the protection we want to give in this movement. Constant practice is required on this—constant checking and constant correction. However, if you use this procedure on the very first day that you attempt to run the guard offense, you will soon find that the boys will get in the habit of lining up just this way. It may be necessary to place the team manager near the position where the forwards line up in the drill and have him correct immediately every boy who does not have his feet properly placed at the beginning of the drill.

We like to do it this way because it gives the man complete ball protection against the defensive man. We want the forward to step out with his inside foot, the body in a crouched position, and on receipt of the pass to turn immediately on the ball of his inside foot and either pass the ball to the pivot man and cut by, or to turn on the ball of his pivot foot and by means of a flip pass (described in Chapter 15, Offensive Guard Play) give the ball to the guard who is cutting by.

We want the same footwork when the forward does not handle the ball but reverses and goes back to the basket. As we have said before, the guards in basketball today crowd the offensive men so tightly that they sometimes have difficulty in getting passes. To loosen up the defensive man it may be necessary to reverse him. We do that in this manner: we have the guard passing into the forward fake a pass to this forward and the forward using the same leading step that he did before step forward with the inside foot. If the guard plays him so strongly that he cannot get the ball, or the guard overcommits himself, we then have this forward (after the initial step has been taken) swing his back leg or the outside leg in behind the guard and, by pivoting on this foot, cut for the basket. The pass may be fed directly to the cutting forward by the guard; or the guard may pass in to the pivot man and the pivot man relay the pass. This same footwork may also be used by the forward on the opposite side of the floor and he can often come in on the blind side, particularly if his guard is one who likes to watch the ball.

We want to eliminate as much false footwork as possible and we want to establish uniformity in our ball handling. The footwork and stance of the defensive player are discussed in Chapter 17, Individual Defense.

In basketball the situations change with every pass of the ball. Players are constantly on the move. We tell our boys that whenever they break or are in motion, to break quickly and never to loaf. Players should know where they are going before they start, and should never jog along the floor with no particular aim in view.

We like to establish uniformity on all of our plays. As we have said before, we try to eliminate all false movements and false ball handling. We want to get into scoring position as quickly as possible and we do not wish to handle the ball with any more passes than are absolutely necessary. If you can set up a play and get a shot after two or three passes—well and good. The fewer attempts to pass the ball, the fewer times you will fumble.

This past season I counted the passes used by one of the finest teams in the country. They passed the ball twenty-eight times in an offensive drive toward the basket and then had a pass intercepted. It was a beautiful exhibition of passing but it was in the end useless.

At first it was somewhat difficult to make our boys understand that if the play is designed to go in on the other side of the floor, unless they are invited to carry out an assignment in that play, they should stay away from the play and be ready for offensive rebounding, or for a quick switch back to defense. Many players have come to us from high school teams that did not have an established pattern of play. When we set up something definite to run, these boys just wander into the situation and often clog up the area where they are not supposed to be. At such times we just stop practice and say, "What are you doing here?" Soon the boys find out they cannot wander around on the floor because our pattern of play calls for specific assignments.

When a boy starts a play, he ought to have definite footwork and he should never leave his position until he is ready to go, and go at full speed. We practice to free a boy by mixing in feinting, shifting, reversing, pivoting, changing of pace, and other measures of deception. "Do not run in straight lines or in circles," is one of the pet phrases of every coach.

Regardless of what system of play is used, the idea is to free a player so that he can score. In the fast break system the idea is to get this advantage by numbers or by speed; in the deliberate offensive system the idea is to get it by means of a screen. When all of the individual players are well drilled in fundamentals and act in harmony, the result is what we call team play.

We tell our boys to study their opponents' faults and keep them in mind in order to take advantage of them. If an opponent is especially weak, we never try to wear out our welcome because we may have need of "cashing in" on his weakness before the game is over. Also, if this player's weakness is taken advantage of too often, a substitute will be in soon to take the place of this particular player. In other words, study your opponent for his weaknesses; as has been said many times, "The team that makes the most mistakes will lose in the end." Each player should be alert and should catalog the weaknesses of his man, all the time thinking and planning. Study the footwork of the opponent. Does he play you close or does he stay away? Can you throw him off balance? How fast is he? Is he a ballhawk? How does he play on defense under the basket? Does he follow the ball and allow you to get away? Can you feint him out of position? Can you throw him off by change of pace? Can you reverse him?

In running, without the ball or dribbling the ball, one of the best methods for getting clear of the defensive man is to vary the speed. In cutting, learn to shorten step or develop full strides as the situation demands. A quick turn in a new direction will often prove to be a good way of losing the defense.

These are all individual responsibilities of team play and, as I have said before, come only from long hours of work on fundamentals. To you boys who are learning the game and to the coaches who are teaching these boys, let me state: Spend your time on fundamentals, for fundamentals are polish. A polished team wins.

9

Getting Possession of the Ball

Before we discuss offensive basketball, it is well to keep in mind the fact that it is necessary to have ball possession before you can score. This statement may seem elementary, but too much importance cannot be attached to it. In our close games, possession of the ball is possibly the determining factor between victory and defeat. Playing a game in the winter of 1948, we were very fortunate in that we were able to cash in almost every time that we had possession of the ball. We looked for a close game, but at the half we had already scored 58 points and had virtually used every man on the team. All games do not run that true to form. I remember that the coach of the opposing team told me after the game that he went down in the dressing room at the half and said to his boys: "You'll have to fight harder for the rebounds. We must get possession of more of those." He was slightly stunned when one of his boys asked him, "Coach, how do you want us to rebound the ones under the Kentucky basket? They all go through."

Ball possession comes from four different sources.

Center-jump

We can get the ball at the beginning of the game and then again at the beginning of the second half by means of the center-jump. Therefore, this opportunity should not be neglected. In stepping into the center ring, the center should watch the line-up of the men in order to enable him to place the tip-off so that one of his own men will get it. We like to have a definite assignment on the tip-off before the game. We like to tip to a tall forward and have him try for a position that will enable him to take one or two steps and then jump high to get the tap. We have in the last few years had boys who have always taken pride in being able to get the tip-off, if it should come in their direction. In fact, they have always said, "Tip the ball to me, I'll get it."

The stance of the center will vary with the individual. It will be best to determine from experience gained in the practice of tipping how your center should stand in the center ring. Usually the knees are bent, the player is on his toes, he keeps his eyes on the ball as it goes up and then he judges his jump accordingly. As he goes up his arm should be straight, he should use the cushions of his three middle fingers to place the ball. He should attempt to tip the ball, arching it slightly, and he can do this nicely if his arm is straight with his fingers extended. Be sure that the center does not slap the ball. He should time his jump and gauge the height of the ball. Timing is the most important element in jumping. He should alight with knees bent, ready to go on the offense or defense. If you should be unfortunate not to have a tall center or one that can get the tip-off, then you should play a defensive tip-off and fight for the ball. This information is discussed elsewhere. The same fundamentals that apply to the center-jump also are used in the held-ball situations. Every player should practice jumping because it enables the team to get positive ball possession.

Held balls

You have an opportunity to get possession of the ball by means of held balls. You should have a different set-up for these. Even with our championship team of 1948, we hit a three weeks' period in January when we were getting only fifty per cent of the jump balls. We knew this was correct as our chart man had the information for us. We spent ten minutes each day for three days on this and gave exact assignments to each man. Immediately we started getting sixty-five per cent of the jump balls.

Free balls

The third method of getting possession of the ball is by getting the loose or free balls. As I have said before, we play aggressively. Our entire system of play, offensively and defensively, is based on aggressiveness. There have been some coaches that have said football and basketball do not go hand in hand. I have not found this to be true. Basketball gives to a football player, ball handling, grace, lightness on feet, and shiftiness. Football gives to a basketball player ruggedness and aggressiveness. We have been fortunate in the past few years in having boys that love to play basketball. Practice has not been work to them but has been a genuine pleasure. They have been aggressive. Three of these boys have picked up more than their share of loose balls. I have seen them leave their feet dozens of times and dive for loose balls and invariably recover them for our team. After one of our games, one of the visiting coaches came to me. He mentioned one of my boys and said, "He got enough loose balls this evening by diving for them on the floor to win the game for you."

Rebounds

The fourth method is by rebounds, offensively and defensively. I have said time and again that you should never take a chance shot at the basket unless there is more than a reasonable opportunity of making it. In too many instances, boys just throw the ball at the basket and hope that it will go in. We have here at the University of Kentucky adopted a very realistic view of our game of basketball.

We like to say this, "I'll get it, let's see who will throw it away." Our chart man keeps track of our rebounds.

This past year Kentucky was one of the leading teams in the nation on rebounds. We had an average of 58 rebounds per game. We emphasized this. We had several tall players; but again Burrow, our center, who is only six feet, six inches—not regarded as being tall in college play—led with an average of 14.4 rebounds per game. Since our opponents averaged only 41.4, it is easy to understand why we outscored our opponents by a margin of 16.1. And it is our belief that the ball possession that we gained in rebounding gave us the opportunity to average this scoring margin.

I cannot emphasize too much to you coaches and to you players the importance of this rebounding. We practice on it for ten-minute periods three times per week. We block out our opposing players and then go for the ball. As we tell our boys, be sure that your man does not get the rebound. Offensively, we still insist that the shooter follow every shot and we like to maintain a three-and-a-half-men offense rebounding strength with one and a half men on the defense. In other words, we like to keep three men on every play offensively and on the board, with the fourth man being ready for the offensive if the opportunity presents itself or the defensive if the situation requires it; the fifth man on every play is strictly a defensive man who stays back in order to protect our basket. Keep this thought foremost in your mind: "He who controls the back-boards, controls the game."

10

Individual Offense

I hesitate to discuss the individual offense, for basketball is essentially a team game. However, an individual must be an offensive threat. The discussion on fundamentals, footwork, shooting, dribbling, pivoting, and the center-jump covers all individual responsibilities of the offensive men. There are, however, a few other requirements.

Every game will present opportunities where an individual has a chance to score without the help of his teammates. Basketball play does not have such a definite pattern that a rigid set of rules on offense can be applied. There are many coaches today who do not believe in a set play or deliberate offense. They believe that the sum total of the individual moves should determine the team play and, therefore, they attempt to make every player as versatile as possible in all phases of the game, allowing him entire freedom in determining what the play situation may be. They believe that players with good sound fundamentals can do better by making their own play situations than by having a play pattern that has been worked out in advance. When you are of this opinion, certainly individual offense should be carefully discussed.

The first requirement of an individual offensive player is that he should have the proper attitude because it will influence the other players. A player should take pride in all of the fundamental details. He should be unselfish. He should help others to score. As soon as this attitude is apparent he will be on the receiving end of many more of the passes than would otherwise be the case.

The second requirement of an individual is that he should be able to get the ball at the first center-jump if he has been assigned to get it. We have been fortunate here at Kentucky in the past few years in that we have had two forwards who have been six feet, four inches, in height. They have taken pride in being able to get the ball at the center-jump. In the dressing room just before game time, when I ask, "Who is going to get the center-jump?" invariably these boys will hold up their hands and say, "Tap it to me, I'll get it."

A player should play in a crouched position. In other words, he should be ready to move forward, backward, or sideways. Too many players, when not in the play, stand flat-footed and present no threat whatever. We tell our boys that regardless of where the ball may be, play low, and keep the defensive man guessing. Do not telegraph the plays or your movements. Fake with your head, with your shoulders, with your feet, and in this way mislead your opponent as to your real purpose.

Time your movements. Do not wander into a situation. Do not move until the opportunity presents itself, and then come fast. Be alert at all times for there may be loose balls that you can pick up during the game.

Have a good change of pace. Use sidesteps, feints, reverses, and pivots in order to get free.

Go to meet all passes. In modern basketball the defensive man plays so tightly that if you wait for the passes, the defensive man will be certain to intercept the ball before it reaches you.

Outguess your defensive man. An offensive man has a tremendous advantage over the defensive man, as the defensive man must always second-guess what the offensive man is attempting to do. That is why individual footwork plays such an important part in basketball.

Do not lose the ball on an offensive drive. Be sure to make every pass good. If a player has been freed and you are in a position to pass to him, be sure that you give him a good pass as that immediately gives your teammates confidence in your ability.

Follow every shot that you take, or that is taken by your teammates unless you have a defensive assignment on that particular play. Hurry back on defense and help to pick up loose men. Do not loaf coming back on the floor after you have attempted a dribble-in shot. There is a possibility that you may have missed. Get back on the floor as quickly as possible for you may be able to help with the rebounding, or you may be able to get in a position so that a teammate can pass out to you for another easy shot.

All of the time that you are playing, catalog your opponent. In other words, study him to see what he is doing and what you may be able to do with him. You may detect a weakness and when the opportunity presents itself, you may be able to cash in on it.

These are all individual responsibilities and if a man is willing to assume these, he should develop into an outstanding player.

11

Screen Plays

In recent years there has been considerable discussion about the screen play in basketball. In the early development of the game this problem did not come up because all the screens of that time were of an accidental nature. However, as the game of basketball has developed, coaches have defined various offensive movements based on the screens. Some of these resulted in contact and, of course, where this contact occurred fouling often resulted.

By screen play we mean nothing more than two or more offensive men working together in such a way that the movement of a defensive man is temporarily interrupted. This may be either a moving screen or a stationary screen. The idea is to impede temporarily the progress of a defensive man who has been assigned to a particular offensive man. This permits the player who is being guarded by the defensive man to become unguarded for a short period of time. In other words, basketball today is so fast that if a defensive man can be thrown off his stride momentarily, then the offensive man will be free to cut for the basket, receive a pass and score.

You will find various types of offenses in basketball depending on the section of the country that you may be in. In the South, until recent years, offenses depending on screen plays were little used. The same has been true of the East where the usual type of offense is known as the "Give and Go." The screen plays undoubtedly received their greatest development in the Middle West. There are still some sections that are relatively free from the screen play where the offense has been built mainly on the fast-breaking attack.

In 1935 the University of Kentucky had a very outstanding team and made its first trip to Madison Square Garden to play New York University which was National Champion that year. Both teams came into the Garden with undefeated records. Kentucky had an outstanding center that year in Leroy Edwards who was eventually named All-American center. Both teams had excellent offense and defense. The meeting was what may be considered one of the first intersectional basketball games, and of course, introduced the University of Kentucky to the Eastern fans.

Edwards was a big center, six feet, five inches, weighing better than two hundred pounds. He was a deadly scorer under the basket. New York University, of course, knew this and would not permit him to get a position under the offensive basket. It was one of the roughest and most rugged exhibitions of pivot play that has ever been shown.

Kentucky's attack was built on a screening type of play. Its plays were perfectly legal in the Middle West and in the South. But as these boys attempted to set up their plays, they were called for screening. Naturally they were thrown off their game and I, as their coach, was at a loss to understand the interpretation of the rule since we had never run into this before. All of our plays were legal as far as we knew.

At the half I went to the official and politely asked him what we were doing that we should not have been doing. The only answer that I got was, "You know what you're doing. It isn't legal." That did not help me a great deal, and it was difficult for me to go into the dressing room and say to my boys: "Our system of play is illegal. Let's figure out a new one between halves." You can't build an offensive system that quickly. So I told my boys to go out and disregard the plays and to just play the best that they could.

The game came down to within eight seconds of the end, tied at 23-23. Kentucky was fouled for screening, New York University making the free throw to win the game. We felt bad about this. I, as their coach, felt that I had taught an illegal system of play to the boys. What were my boys to think of me for bringing them to the biggest arena in America only to find that I had been teaching them something that was not proper? As far as I knew, everything that I had taught them was perfectly legitimate and was also being taught in every section of the United States outside of the New York City area.

The newspapers made a terrific story of the game. In fact, the controversy raged for the remainder of the year and finally came to the Rules Meeting. Movies of the game were shown at the meeting and the play of the pivot man under the basket was so rugged that it shocked the coaches who saw it. It was not only true in our game but it was true all over the United States. The three-second rule was put in that year to force the pivot man away from the basket, and the screening rule was given its first long session of housecleaning. The veterans in the coaching profession spent hours discussing the rules and some of the finest coaches in America were of the opinion that the rules as interpreted in New York were wrong; the Eastern coaches were of the same opinion in regard to the Western interpretation.

Even at a recent N.C.A.A. Tournament in New York some officials were calling screening fouls, while other officials permitted exactly the same plays to go by unmolested. Since there is still such a great difference in screening and in the interpretation of the rules, we feel that all screens should be known by our boys.

Even today there is some difference in the interpretation of screening in the United States. In the 1955–56 season we were called twice for illegal screening. Both of these screens were called in intersectional games with Eastern teams by Eastern officials. When we play in the Eastern section of the United States we start to get ready for the games at least two weeks in advance by loosening up on our screens in our scrimmage sessions.

I feel that it is the duty of a coach to meet intelligently such a situation. When we play in the Middle West, the screens can be closer. We do not believe in contact on these screens and have never believed in it, and we believe that a coach should design his plays so that contact will not result. It is merely inviting a foul. In all of our plays, whether the screen plays as shown here or the plays that are used in our general system of floor play, there is no attempt to make contact.

We here at the University of Kentucky play teams from every section of the country, and it is, therefore, necessary for our boys to be acquainted with every type of offensive screen maneuver. I have drawn up some of these screen plays from the very simple to the more complex.

In this brief analysis of screen play, I have merely tried to show

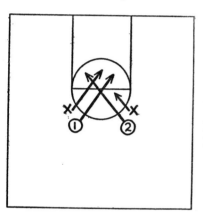

Chart 4. This is a simple maneuver in which two men cooperate in order to pick off a defensive man. It is a simple crisscross in which No. 1 maneuvers his man in such a way that No. 2, by excellent timing, is able to screen off his defensive man on No. 1 as both of them cut for the basket.

Chart 5. No. 1 passes to No. 2. No. 2 dribbles toward the basket, his defensive man following. No. 1 times his movement in such a way that he maneuvers his defensive man into No. 2, who has pivoted and placed himself in the path of the defensive man on No. 1. No. 2 hands No. 1 the ball and goes for the basket.

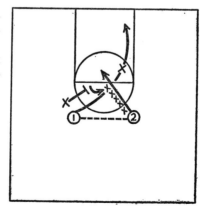

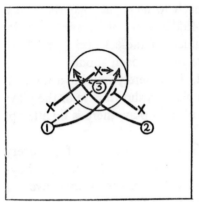

Chart 6. Nos. 1 and 2 have invited a third man, No. 3, into the play. No. 1 passes to No. 3 and cuts by him. No. 3 gives him the pass if he is open. It is assumed that the defensive man on No. 1 will take No. 3. Therefore, No. 2 has timed his movements so that he will cut directly behind No. 1 as he is cutting for the basket, screening off his defensive man so that No. 2 can receive the ball and go to the basket unguarded.

Chart 7. This chart shows the "Inside Screen." No. 1 passes to No. 2; No. 2 passes to No. 3. The pass from No. 2 must be made to No. 3 before the screener No. 1 takes his position on the inside of the defensive man on No. 2. No. 2 cuts behind No. 1, and it is assumed that the defensive man on No. 1 will shift to take No. 2. If that is the case, then No. 1 is inside of the defensive man that was guarding No. 2, and he goes in toward the basket and receives a pass from No. 3.

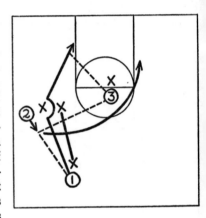

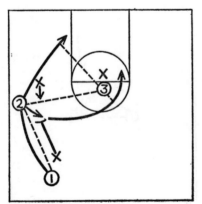

Chart 8. The "Guard Around Play." No. 1 passes to No. 2. No. 2 passes to No. 3. No. 1 cuts in with his pass to No. 2 as a screen, cutting so close to him that the defensive man on No. 1 does not have a clear path in order to stay with No. 1. No. 1 receives the pass from No. 3 as he cuts toward the basket.

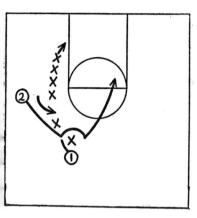

Chart 9. The "Back Screen." No. 2 goes across and takes his position behind the defensive man on No. 1. The defensive man on No. 2 will go with him. No. 1 swings around his defensive man and dribbles toward the basket as the defensive man on No. 2 shifts to take No. 1. Then No. 2 will cut for the basket and take a pass from No. 1. In either case, No. 2 is behind the defensive man on No. 1 and has an inside position on him toward the basket.

Chart 10. The play known as the "Guard Across." This chart shows another variation of the screen. No. 1 passes to No. 3 and, as he does so, he cuts behind the defensive man on No. 2. No. 2 times his movements in such a way that, as soon as the screen is closed, he cuts for the basket. The idea is to pocket the defensive man on No. 2. No. 1 and No. 2 then take the paths indicated in the diagram, and No. 3 passes to one of them.

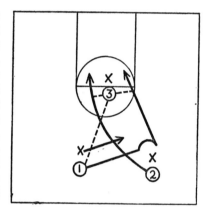

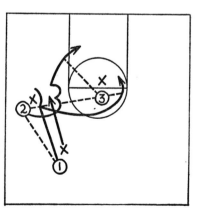

Chart 11. The "Double" or "Roll Screen." No. 1 passes to No. 2 and goes on the inside to screen the defensive man on No. 2. No. 2 passes to No. 3, rolls out of the screen, and cuts around No. 1. No. 1 cuts for the basket if he is on the inside of the defensive man on No. 2. No. 3 can then pass to either No. 1 or No. 2, depending on which is free.

Chart 12. The "Side Screen," usually used in a continuity type of offense or as a screen between the center and forward. No. 1 screens the defensive man on No. 2. No. 2 cuts for the basket. It is assumed that the defensive man on No. 1 will pick up No. 2. If that is the case, No. 1 will be open because he has an inside position on the defensive man that originally was on No. 2. This is sometimes known also as a "Lateral Screen."

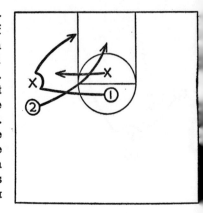

some of the more commonly used screens in today's modern basketball. It is highly important that all of the men on the team understand these screens so that they will know not only how to execute them but also how to guard against them defensively. It is also desirable for them to understand these so that when time out is called and they talk about the various movements of their opponents, they will all understand exactly what they are discussing. We discuss all of these screens during the early part of the year, and use ball-handling drills to acquaint our boys with the proper methods of shifting and guarding against them. As a result, when we go into the dressing room between halves and talk about the various types of screens used by our opponents, our boys fully understand what we are talking about. It is essential that a well trained basketball player today have a complete understanding of these screens in order that he may intelligently guard against them during a game.

12

Seven Cardinal Principles of Offensive Play

Let me say, to begin with, that there are no secrets in basketball. There are coaches who, when the principles of basketball are explained to them, do not find the answers sufficiently intellectual to be satisfying. These same individuals, when a chemistry teacher tells them that the formula for water is two parts hydrogen and one part oxygen, don't complain that the formula is unsophisticated. But unfortunately, many of them turn up their noses at the basic truths of basketball, because these truths are too commonplace.

Too many coaches today do not realize that a shot chart is the best index of how a game has been played; and very few coaches really get the value from the shot chart that they should. Too many coaches use the shot chart just as a record for the collection of statistics, and they do not go into the meaning of this chart sufficiently to get the true value out of it. As is well known, we were possibly the first school in America to make extensive use of the shot chart; and practically all of the statistics that are kept today were kept in our files and used by us for some fifteen years.

There are *Seven Cardinal Principles* that are important in offensive play. In going over these principles it will be possible for everyone to understand why we place so much emphasis on the shot chart and why we are able to discuss a game intelligently after it is over. Peculiar as it may seem, one's memory is not always too good. Very often you may *think* that one of your boys has played a very outstanding game. But when you consult the shot chart you will be able to *see* whether or not your memory has played tricks on you, and whether or not you have the exact picture as it is revealed by the chart. We believe that these seven things are most important:

1. Get the position shot

We have believed that every player on a team has certain shots that are peculiar to his position. In beginning our shooting drills we divide our boys into forwards, guards, and centers, and try to give them a basket where each group can work alone. In watching teams warm up or practice I have been amazed at the indifferent shooting that teams employ. I have watched a center take a shot from thirty feet out and spend practically all of the warm up drill out at that position. Correct shooting practice drills are essential.

A guard must learn to hit from the floor from four positions at least twenty feet out. He must learn to drive at the basket and shoot a lay-up shot. He must learn to drive at the basket, stop, and use a jump shot. Shots are of two varieties: those from a standing position and those from an in-motion position. The guard must be able to use all of them.

A forward should learn to shoot from his side of the floor and concentrate all of his efforts on that side. He should learn to shoot from a position near the side of the floor where an extension of the free-throw line would cross. He should learn to drive with a dribble across in front of the pivot man, to jump, and to shoot. He should learn to drive and go around the pivot man all the way and use a lay-up shot. He should learn to reverse with the ball from his original position, drive for the basket, go all the way, or to be able to stop and use the jump shot.

The pivot man should work in the area out from the basket to a position about twelve or fifteen feet out. Every shot peculiar to the pivot man should be taught. If the pivot man can shoot well from out on the floor this should be encouraged, since usually the defensive man who guards the pivot man does not like to go out that far. Few pivot men are good long shots; but they certainly should be encouraged to make hook shots, turn-around shots, jump shots, and fade-away shots.

In other words, concentrate on getting good shots for the positions to which the boys are assigned, and you will be surprised at how your percentage will increase.

2. Get the long shot

You have often heard it said that, if a boy can't shoot crips and get lay-up shots, he is not a sound ballplayer. I have often heard coaches say that they lost a game because a boy missed a lay-up in the last few seconds of play. I wonder whether the game was really lost because of that, or whether it was lost because a guard was permitted to shoot from twenty feet out and missed all of his shots, allowing the opponents to get the ball. If you have a team that can't shoot long, it will be difficult to get the short shot, because the defense will concentrate under the basket and not permit you to work a play so that you can get a short shot. If you can hit from out on the floor, it will be necessary for the defense to cover you; and then, when the defense covers for a long shot, you will be able to get the ball in to the pivot man and set up a screening play so that you can get the short shots. With the defense tight, your fast men will be able to make use of their speed and run past the defensive men. That is why it is so important to have a long shooter on the team. You should work at least thirty minutes a day on the long shot, on passing in to the pivot man, and on quickly cutting for the basket for a lay-up shot. It takes constant practice to perfect aim and precision in shooting baskets.

3. Get the over shot

By getting the over shot we mean that you must get the shot over the screener. You can do this either by passing the ball in to your teammate and having him set a screen for you, permitting you to shoot from the outside or over him, or by throwing the ball to your teammate and establishing a screen, permitting him to shoot over you. This over shot can easily be set up, especially against floating defenses; and, unless the defense is very aggressive, the over shot will be easy to get.

4. Get the second shot

Far too often a team will take a shot at the basket and lose possession. It can be very difficult for this team to win. This is especially true when the defense floats badly or uses a zone. In either case you must so design your offensive maneuvers that you will have a maximum amount of rebounding strength on the boards. This will permit you to get possession of the ball and get the second shot or the third and fourth shots, before you surrender the ball to the opponents.

I watched a game in the winter of 1955 in which it was very evident as to what was taking place. Team A realized that Team B had very indifferent long shooters on its team. Team A floated badly. It allowed the shooters to take unlimited shots at the basket and that usually ended the offensive movement, since Team A immediately got the rebound. Team B was a very fine team under ordinary conditions, but it couldn't get the second shot from its offense. It was apparent that Team B could not get its rebounding strength to the basket, because Team A was not only making use of its strategy, but was blocking out the offensive rebounders of Team B. After the game the coach of Team B said, "We got a lot of good shots, but couldn't hit." That wasn't the case. The shots were good but were taken by indifferent shooters; and the entire theory of Team A was to get possession of the ball after the first shot. It is important to check your offense to make sure that you are getting the second shot or additional shots.

5. Get the percentage shot

As I have mentioned before, there is too much indifferent shooting on teams. The shots should be taken by the boys who are the best percentage shooters. If a boy can shoot and hit 40 per cent of his shots, it's a cinch that he is taking good shots and that he has the ability to make a high percentage of his attempts. There are other boys who will attempt as many shots but only hit 20 per cent of them. The shot chart will immediately tell the coach exactly which boy is doing the most shooting and which boy is hitting the biggest percentage of shots. Certainly it makes a lot of difference from which position on the floor these shots are taken; but the fact still remains that you should work to get shots that will give you the best percentage. If a boy is shooting 35 per cent or better from the floor, and if the defense permits him to take good shots from there, he should be permitted to shoot from that position unless he can pass to a teammate who has a better position. The highest percentages of shots are usually made by the tall men near the basket. They have a shorter distance to shoot, and on rebound shots their size will usually permit them to increase the percentage of their shooting.

In going over these first five cardinal principles, your shot chart will tell you whether your boys have the ability to get the long shots. It will also tell you whether or not you have sufficient rebounding strength to get the second shot. If you have a big pivot man who can knock in attempts that are missed from out on the floor, then you will have an excellent opportunity not only for setting up a dangerous offense, but also for getting the second shot and for taking advantage of the percentage. If the long shot fails to develop, then the coach should so design his offense as to use the maximum amount of time to work the ball in to the pivot man, in order to increase the percentage on shooting.

6. Take out the floater

We have had tremendous difficulty in the last ten years with floating defenses; and I can assure you that we have worked as hard on these as on almost any phase of the game. Our offense is set up as a single post offense. We do not care to argue about the merits of this with anyone, for we have established in our own minds that this is the best offense for us. We have given it tremendous study, we know a lot about it, and it is giving us the results that we are seeking. We have been the "spread team" of the nation for many years—that is, the spread between offense and defense—and our theory has always been that this is the soundest basketball. Lowness of score does not indicate the defensive ability of a team, but the margin by which you beat a team does indicate your defensive strength. The best way to cure a floating defense is to have excellent long shooters. If the boys can hit from out on the floor there will be little danger of the opponents' dropping in on the pivot man and clogging up the offense. Since we play this single pivot offense, we have designed our plays so that a floater may be taken out of play and all of our plays run just exactly as though the defense were tight.

7. Control the ball

In one of our shot chart columns we keep strict account of the number of times we lose control of the ball and exactly how we lose it. Nothing is more deplorable than to fight viciously to regain the ball and then take it down in your own offensive territory, walk with it, have it intercepted, throw it out of bounds, or have the pivot man stand in the three-second area too long, or in some other way lose control before you get the shot. We like to design our plays so that by a minimum of ball handling we get a shot at the basket. We believe that every time a ball is passed there is danger of losing it; therefore, we want to handle it as infrequently as possible and then get the shot as quickly as possible—with one thing in mind, and that is perfect ball control.

A few years ago, in a game played against us, a team tried ball control. They passed the ball eighteen times and then threw it out of bounds. I sat there amazed, for we already had a 30-point lead and I couldn't understand the motive behind this type of offense. This is not ball control. By ball control we mean keeping the ball and getting a good opportunity to score with a well-defined play.

In early-season play let me again emphasize the necessity of establishing uniformity in all phases of play, with particular emphasis on individual skills. Many boys have individual abilities that they have acquired down through the years; and it is possible for them to do one or more particular things differently or better than other boys. These boys should not be deprived of using these individual skills, but they should be developed and encouraged to fit into team play. In early-season play try to establish individual skills by watching:

1. Stance of players.
2. Floor position.
3. Footwork.
4. Self control in men.
5. Timing and uniformity.

These also are some often overlooked playing requirements:

1. Speed.
2. Leg spring.
3. Endurance.

Watch particularly the latter. If a team does not have the proper endurance qualities, all the other phases of basketball will go out the window when the heat is applied during the closing minutes of the ballgame.

13

Team Offense

Early in his career a coach should establish in his mind a general system of team play that he feels is the best, and then he should develop that particular style to its maximum strength. There are, perhaps, as many styles of basketball as there are coaches coaching the game. Any organization of play, regardless of how simple or how complex, is a system.

Several years ago I knew of a team that was regarded as one of the finest in scholastic play. Try as hard as one might, it was impossible to figure out the pattern of offense or defense that this team employed. There were six boys on this team and with the system that they had made up among themselves, they were able to defeat the best coached and organized teams in the state. This team went on to college and played together as a unit. When their college coach substituted other players into the team, it just wouldn't function. The coach, himself, tried to figure out what made this particular team click and, after three years of watching them play together, he finally stated that he had discovered the secret of their success.

"They don't know how to play and they won't let anyone else play."

Despite that, the boys got along well together. They had merely worked out a system whereby they understood each other. That is important in team play.

Every coach is looking for five regulars. He should get them together as quickly as possible and when he is satisfied that he has the right combination he should not be quick in breaking them up. He should not be too much interested in listening to outside coaching and criticism. After all, a barber is still a better hair cutter than coach.

General principles of team play

We here at the University like to think any system of offense or defense should be aggressive. We do not like to play a slow, deliberate, sure game. We like to take chances. That is the very spirit of aggressive play and is the spirit of modern youth. That is the spirit of our pioneer forefathers. The pilgrims who landed at Plymouth Rock did not look for security. What security did Daniel Boone ask for when he penetrated the wilderness, and what security did our pioneer mothers and fathers have when they carved their homes out of the western plains? It is true that we make a lot of mistakes but we believe that unless we make too many, our aggressive style will win for us. We play fast ball, and believe that a team can have just as much organization and possibly more in this style of game than with the deliberate style. Our boys like to play it and it is the attempt of this chapter to give an exact picture of our system of play.

Besides the spirit of aggressiveness, our next requirement is complete mastery of details or fundamentals. We wish to establish uniformity in these, and we want perfect agreement in their execution. We do not believe in hope passes; we want our passes so thrown that they fit perfectly into a pattern of play.

The next requirement is that of speed. Naturally, we are seeking boys who are fast but we also want to teach them how to execute a fast pass, how to get into offensive position as fast as possible, and how to get back into defensive position also as speedily as possible. We want them to have speed in execution of all plays with as few passes as possible.

Coordination is the next requirement. In any system of play a coordinated pattern should be established. Players should have the proper relationship, so that when an offensive man makes a move, he can do so with complete assurance that one of his teammates will be back to handle the defensive assignment. All movements of the team should be organized. The fast break should be well understood and should not be just a helter-skelter attack for the basket. On out-of-bounds play, everyone should understand perfectly what his assignments are. We like to have the same man handle all the balls on out-of-bounds with the screening assignments for the remainder of the men well understood by all.

From this naturally grows the fact that we have indicated throughout the book, that our offense after our fast break attack is of a mechanical nature. We do not believe that an offense can be effective if it is left to chance. We have a set of plays off our pivot post offense that are absolutely mechanical in their execution. Everybody on the team knows exactly what we are going to do in our offensive move as soon as we cross the center line.

Our plays are numbered and the reason for this is twofold. One is that the players can call out the numbers to each other and in that way definitely let each other know what play is being run. Secondly, it enables us to discuss the plays intelligently when talking with each other. When we come into the dressing room at the half, one of the boys may say to me, "Coach, we can run number five." Instantly, every boy knows exactly what we are talking about. When we go out to work on our plays in the practice sessions and we feel that a certain pattern needs to be reviewed, everyone on the squad knows immediately what our assignment is at that particular time.

If you have an organized system of play you definitely need to follow a mechanical pattern. In teaching this mechanical style of play it is necessary for the boys to have confidence in the system. Naturally, the plays must all be flexible and have variations and

checks. If a defense shifts, a play must have a check for that particular assignment. But in our style of basketball we know exactly
where every pass is going the minute the play starts. This places
responsibility on the offensive pattern because if a play is not executed properly we can immediately put our finger on the fault. The
boys like to play this kind of game as they all understand what they
are supposed to do. In the freedom system, or in that style where
boys make their plays as they go along according to their own
judgment, it is hard to trace the responsibility for a play's failure
to work.

I feel that we are fortunate here at the University in that we have
built a fine tradition in basketball. Down through the years it has
been the outstanding sport at this institution. This tradition has developed tremendous pride in our teams and in our boys so that they
try to look as good as the teams that have preceded them.

We do not believe that any defensive work should be taught until
the offensive pattern has been fairly well mastered and established.
In fact, we do not work defensively in the first three or four weeks
of practice. We feel that if we place a tough defense on the offense
at the very beginning, the boys will not have as complete confidence
in the plays as they will have if they are enabled to run them without too much opposition. This gives immediate confidence in our
system to the new boys, and it is important to keep them coming
along.

Qualifications of the players in team play

In today's basketball we do not have guards and forwards like
those of several years ago when the idea of the forward was to
score and the responsibility of a guard was to prevent the opponents
from scoring. Early in our play we had a "running forward," a
"standing forward," a "standing guard," and a "running guard."
It is difficult today to tell what a forward ought to do and what a
guard ought to do because in the continuity type of offense every
player is a constant scoring threat and fits into the play in exactly
the same manner as any other man on the team. We still, in our
style of play, like to have forwards, guards, and centers. This is
what we look for in men playing the various positions.

Forward. It is still always better to have a good big man than a good little man, although ability does not necessarily come with size. In the 1955–56 season we had four forwards who were six feet, five inches in height. One of the forwards was six feet, three inches. Our center was six feet, six inches, and our five guards were five feet, eleven inches, to six feet, three inches. That gave us exactly the material we like for a team. Almost every forward could play in the pivot.

If you can get one good, big forward who is a good shot, quick on his feet, clever with his hands, who thinks well, who can possibly move into the pivot position, who has courage, and who can rebound well, you are fortunate. The other forward need not be as large and if you have a smaller man with tremendous speed, a boy who can think and react quickly, who can reverse and can shoot well, he will meet the requirements of the other forward.

Guard. A good guard in present-day basketball must not only be a good guard but also a good offensive player. As you will see in Chapter 15, Offensive Guard Play, we have nine basic plays for our guards in sequence. A guard is a quarter-back on the team in our style of play. He must know when to make a pass, where to make a pass, and when to withhold it from play. In the past two years one of our guards has been the second leading scorer, only second to our center. Two years prior to this time one of our guards was the leading scorer.

Successful teams today must have a pair of guards who can start the plays and who alternate in the offense as the fourth man or the fifth man depending entirely on which play is being run. As will be seen when our floor plays are explained, there are times when both of our guards are in on the same play while one of our forwards will be back for defensive work.

The ideal combination is to have guards with size, who are fast, aggressive, good dribblers and accurate shots. They should be able to shoot long with accuracy. If both guards are excellent long shots it will prevent the defense from sinking against your offensive forwards and center, and it will give you an opportunity to set your screening plays. A guard playing offensive must have courage to stay under the basket to fight for rebounds. He must not allow the opponents to drive him out from under the basket but must be able to stand his ground at all times. He must be able to get the ball off the boards and pass out quickly or dribble it over to the side of the floor away from the danger zone and then pass it out. He should have leg spring to enable him to get up in the air for the rebounds.

Dribbling plays an important part in the offensive work of a guard. He is usually required to bring the ball up to the center of the floor where the first line of the opposition will be met. He should be able to protect this ball from charging opponents. If he can go all the way with his dribble, he should do so. If not, he should stop near the center line, wait until all of his teammates are in their correct positions, and then start his offensive play. He should not telegraph his pass either with his eyes or with the ball, but should be just as deceptive as possible in getting the ball in to his teammates by means of head fakes, body fakes, or fakes with the ball. A good guard should not be a ball-hawk but should be able to meet all the requirements of good individual defensive play. We are now primarily interested in the requirements of an all-around guard.

Center. The center is really the important cog in the average modern basketball team. In addition to the unusual physical qualifications, he must possess the essential fundamentals that are found both in the guard and in the forward. The ability to handle the ball is the first important requirement of a good center; to excel, he must have height.

Centers may be used differently by some coaches but we like to think of an ideal center in terms of six feet, five inches or better, weighing approximately two hundred pounds. Naturally, if you can get them taller than this, so much the better, but it is our opinion that a six feet, five inch, boy should be able to handle himself well enough to take care of almost any situation. Unfortunately, this is not true of many of our big men today; they have played through high school where due to the fact that they were six feet, five inches or more, they have stood around flat-footed because most of the men they played with were much smaller than they. They were not forced to jump, and jumping in a center is one of the essential requirements.

In the very opening play at the center-jump, a center should get the ball for his team. He has at least two opportunities in each game to get the ball at center and this may mean the difference between victory and defeat. It is the accumulation of the little things during a game that beats you. The big things never do because if they are big factors, you are usually beaten to begin with. So, these two center-jumps should be controlled by your center.

The reason we want a center with weight is that a lighter man is too easily moved away from under the basket in offensive and defensive territory. A good center should be able to control both boards by tapping in balls on his offensive boards and by taking the ball off the defensive board and passing it out quickly.

Since we play our center in the pivot, we will now discuss the mechanics of the pivot play and that will give the other individual responsibilities of a good center.

Mechanics of the pivot play

There are several ways that the man playing on the pivot may assume his position. In some games the opposing defensive man will not give him a great deal of opposition and, if this is the case, he can line up in front of the free-throw line and handle the ball without interference. However, that is not always the case, and the pivot man may have to fight his way in, in order to arrive at a position where he can catch the ball and repass it to a teammate. We tell our centers to hurry and get down for the play as quickly as possible because our offense, to a large extent, depends on them. If a center meets a great deal of opposition on the free-throw line, he may have to go back near the basket and run out to meet the pass. The guard should then be sure to get the pass in to him so that the ball and the pivot man will arrive at the free-throw line at approximately the same time. It is useless for a pivot man to fight his way out to the free-throw line and then not get the ball immediately. If the ball is not passed in at precisely the exact time, the defensive man will be there to bother the pivot man again, and you have exactly the same situation that you tried to get away from when the pivot man moved back to the base line and then came out. The play off the pivot man works smoothly if all of these passes are synchronized.

It may be necessary for the pivot man to move down the side of the floor, reverse his man, and then go to the free-throw line. As we tell our centers, it is impossible to establish a definite pattern for this. All defensive men play differently and you must play to the weakness of your particular man; that will best tell you how to establish your position.

A pivot man should be light on his feet. He should be cool; he should have good hands. He should be able to pass the ball and to hold it expertly; he should be able to pass flawlessly and accurately to cutting teammates. He must have excellent judgment in knowing when to pass the ball, in knowing when to hold it, and when to pass it back out, when to reverse and go in for a shot himself, and when to step out and take a pet mechanical or jump shot.

The footwork of this pivot man is important. Some men like to stand with their feet together, their legs straight, body only slightly crouched, back straight, head up, arms out. This stance makes an extremely good target for the ball passer. In addition it gives the pivot man excellent protection, as a defensive man is not able to reach the ball as easily as when the pivot man is crouched. However, some players prefer to keep one foot slightly ahead of the other, bend over as far as possible, and reach for the ball. In the former position, a high pass is usually thrown to the pivot man. In the latter, a floor bounce is used. It is best to throw in a floor bounce in front of the pivot man. We use a quick baseball pass or a one-handed underhand pass in passing the ball from our forwards at the side of the floor to the pivot man, our pivot man standing with his hands stretching out to indicate where he wishes to receive the ball. It may be necessary for him to take a small shuffle jump to that particular side to be sure of getting the pass, or he may wish to take a step or two out to meet it, particularly if the ball comes in directly from the front. The hands should be outstretched in both cases with the hands alone catching the ball. A good pivot man should be able to pass the ball from this position with a small wrist flip. However, if he is not able to make a pass immediately and the defensive man is playing directly behind him, he should bring the ball in directly in front of his body. He should then watch the arms of the opposing defensive man; if the defensive man makes a fight to get the ball and extends his arms over the shoulders, the pivot man should make a one-handed underhand pass or floor bounce to a teammate cutting to the basket. If the defensive man's arms are below the pivot man's arms he can then make a one-handed overhand pass. A pivot man here must keep his head up. He must be able to watch for his teammates cutting in to the basket.

In our series of plays we attempt to free a man by means of one screen or two screens and because we like to play a mechanical game, our pivot man knows exactly where and when to pass the ball. We tell our boys never to pass the ball in to the pivot man unless they plan to cut off of him. Do not worry the pivot man with the ball unless a play develops. Keep the ball out on the floor until you are ready to run a play. All passes thrown in to the pivot man from the side should be thrown as far in front of him as he can reach because a defensive man may be crowding him and knock the ball away. Again, the footwork will largely be determined by the pressure that is put on the pivot man by the defending man.

If the pivot man is not able to give a pass to a man cutting by, he has two other options. The first is to pass the ball out on the floor so that the play can be reorganized and run again. The second option is an opportunity for him to score. In our system of play he is essentially a feeder. We are of the opinion that too many pivot men take chance shots at the basket when they should be passing off or passing out. However, a good pivot man should sense when he is open and, if a defensive man is playing him strongly to one side he should, by means of a dribble or a slide dribble, go in to the basket and score. By slide dribble we mean that he goes back to the basket and instead of using a one-step pivot jump, he slides both feet as he takes the dribble and then takes off with the foot nearest the basket. He may be able to fake the ball in such a way that the defensive man will go for it and he can then dive under him and go in and score. It may be possible for him to use a jump shot by jumping in the air, turning, and using a two-handed shot or flip shot that is described in Chapter 5 under "Shooting." It may be possible for him to take a dribble away to the side of the floor and take a one-handed or two-handed shot from there. Again, the way the defensive man plays the pivot man will determine exactly how he should play that position.

That is why we say that it is highly important for a pivot man to have a well-defined sense of judgment, that he must keep cool, and that he must be able to handle the ball well under pressure.

As has been said before, the sum of the individual movements goes to make the team system. As the individual functions, so does the team. It will be impossible to discuss here in detail the various systems of play, so only a complete setup of the Kentucky system will be given.

We think that a coach ought to think out clearly his style of play and then stick to that style if the theory is sound. To be theoretically right, however, isn't sufficient. He must also be practically right. The theory on which the University of Kentucky play is based is the same that my teams have been using for the past twenty-six years with minor changes here and there from year to year to take into consideration the changes in the rules, changes in material, and changes gained from experience. This theory of play has been fairly kind to us, and until we are convinced that there is a better system, we will stick to the one we have. Our boys all know our system, it is fairly simple, and we are getting results; so we see no need of changing.

This past season we had two tip-off play variations, four out-of-bound plays, ten basic floor plays with variations, and a fast break setup. The guard fundamental offensive drill is considered as only one play, although there are nine different ways that a guard and forward may execute it. We found that two tip-off plays proved sufficient and we put more of a premium on out-of-bounds plays for there we had actual possession of the ball. We arranged our defense in such a manner as to give our fastest men an advantage on breaking for the basket whenever we gained control of the ball. Our first pass-out was long in order to cut off as many defensive men as possible. Then, by means of our setup which varies, we broke for the basket in a quick attempt to score. We used a fast break if we could get two men down on one defensive man, or three men on two defensive men. This proved very effective, and we scored a lot of baskets because the defense was unable to pick us up in time. In all fairness we should say that we probably had on the squad two of the fastest men that we have had for years. If we failed to have a fast break, we advanced the ball over the center line and then used our set plays to score. This system of play has all the essential ingredients of the game; namely, speed, lightning passes, dribbling, cutting, faking, change of pace, and above all, *action*. That's what the customers pay for.

We believe that we can say that we have been fairly successful with this system, for our team, in the past four seasons, has scored an average of 82.3 against our opponents' 55.4, for an average scoring margin of 26.9; 88.5 against our opponents' 60.5, for an average scoring margin of 28; 76.5 against our opponents' 61.8, for an average scoring margin of 14.7; and an average of 84.5 against our opponents' 69.3, for an average scoring margin of 15.2. As we have said before, it is the scoring margin by which you defeat a team that is the determining factor in your defensive play.

14

Fast Break

There has been much discussion in recent years of the fast break in basketball. At one time it was the principal scoring threat used by all teams. Then for a period the slower or mechanical type of game came into being, and the fast break was virtually eliminated by most of the better teams. Recently, however, the fast break has come back again and today is the principal scoring threat employed by most of the better teams.

In fact, the game has become much faster in the past few years and it is not unusual for a team to have a season scoring average of seventy-five points or more. These big averages, which have come about because of the fast break, have increased the spectators' interest in the sport so that today, all over America, many schools lack a gymnasium or field house large enough to accommodate the persons who wish to see the games.

Fast play is important because basketball is essentially a game of action. In the slow or mechanical game that prevailed a number of years ago, action was eliminated to a large extent. It has been our feeling that people pay to see action. In other words, if no one comes to see what you are doing, you aren't getting much done.

There are three schools of thought on the fast break. There are those who believe that the more deliberate the type of offense, the sounder it is, owing to the fact that the fast break tends to cause carelessness in ball handling and rules out careful planning of the attack. Another school maintains that the fast break is the best scoring play in basketball and should be used whenever an opportunity presents itself. Then there is a third school of thought which believes that it is well to mix the two styles of play, and that by so doing the best attack can be presented. We are of the opinion that the last-mentioned method fits into our style of play the best. The fast break is effective because it enables a team to score before the defense has had an opportunity to get set. Therefore, it is not necessary for a team always to work through a completely organized defense. A fast break, if used properly, will tend to discourage a well organized attack.

There are several methods of employing the fast break, and a coach may have to adapt these to the material available. In order to have a fast break, you must practice it constantly. At first it will appear as a helter-skelter offensive, and unless a definite pattern is established, it may tend to become exactly that.

If the fast break should not be successful, then the players move into their regular offensive positions and start their deliberate game immediately.

The accompanying charts suggest fast-break attacks.

As described under Chart 15 Rhode Island plays a percentage game after free throws. This is how we played them in the finals of the National Invitational Tournament in 1946:

We played our players No. 1 and No. 2 on their outlying men in such a position that they were slightly in front of them. Should we have played behind them, we felt that our opponents would have been in an excellent position to get the outlet pass. No. X3 was usually Calverley, voted the outstanding man in the tournament. He played out, away from our free-thrower in such a position that,

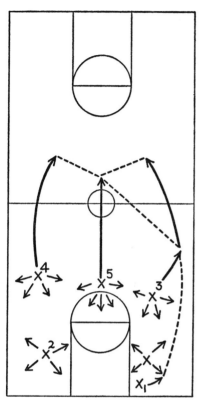

Chart 13. The fast break off a zone defense with two big men playing back. Player No. 1 has taken the ball and has thrown it out to Forward No. 3, who has started to break for the basket. Player No. 5, who plays in the center of the front line, immediately has started to break down the center of the floor after seeing that No. 1 has the ball. No. 3 turns and passes to No. 5, who dribbles down the floor or passes to No. 3 or 4 as the opportunity presents itself.

after the free throw, the thrower would have difficulty in getting to him. The reason for this was explained to us after the game. They wanted to keep this man at such a distance from the free-thrower that it would tend to worry the man at the line. This distance was great enough that the free thrower would have difficulty in covering the player X3 after the throw. If the players at positions X1 and X2 were covered the pass, naturally, would come out to X3. By worrying the free-thrower they felt it made him pull his throws.

Calverley was exceedingly fast, and after receiving the pass, came directly down the middle of the floor with both of the men in advance of him timing their movements in such a way that all three of them presented a terrific problem to our two men who were back.

We felt that if we could stop Rhode Island's fast break (which had averaged eighty-three points per game for that entire season), we would have an excellent chance to win. We told our boys

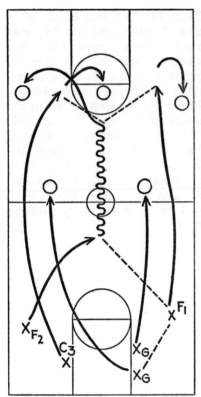

Chart 14. The setup employed by most teams on a defensive free throw. It is the one used also at the University of Kentucky. The guard takes the ball off the backboard and passes out to forward, F1. The opposite forward, F2, cuts to the center of the floor to receive a pass from F1. He dribbles down the center and then passes to F1 or to Center C3, who has cut in the lines indicated on the chart. If the fast break should be successfully stopped, the players are still in a position to take their regular places in the pivot post offense without losing a great deal of time. The chart shows this position.

before the game that if we could hold them to forty-five points, we could win. We held them to exactly forty-five points, but little thought that we would score only forty-six. However, on this particular occasion, it was exactly enough.

Eastern style of play

The Eastern style of play is referred to at times as the "give and go." It is also called the "five-man offense." It is based primarily on individual ability to handle the ball, keeping the entire team in motion until the opportunity presents itself for one of the players to get a fast and uninterrupted cut for the basket. Every player on the team must be a good ball handler as all must move with equal facility in the offensive pattern. Each player is also a potential scorer. In passing the ball to a teammate the player may cut in

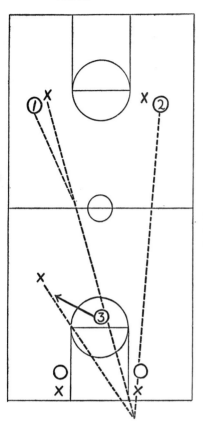

Chart 15. The Rhode Island fast break after a free throw. They figure that any team will make six out of ten free throws. That gives them possession of the ball six out of ten times. It will be necessary to keep two men back to cover their outlying men, which will enable only two opponents to be under the basket to fight for a missed free throw. Since they have two men back, it gives them two chances out of four to get the rebound. Rhode Island figures to get the ball in eight out of every ten such situations.

front or behind the man passed to. If he cuts behind, he usually gets a short flip pass in return. If he goes in front he will attempt to cut for the basket, if open, and receive a pass from the man to whom he passed as he cuts for the basket. Hence, the term "give and go."

This system takes into consideration individual skills. Thus, a player who has individual ability can make use of it. If he is good, he will look good. In the mechanical style of game where the perfect timing and execution of the play is the thing, a brilliant individual may not shine as brilliantly. Players who know each other's style of play often pair up in making pet plays. Players who have been coached on different teams employing the same style of play may be played on the same team and operate as a unit if the pattern is the same. In other words, the players weave in and out, go deep into the corners, turn and come back out, receiving passes and

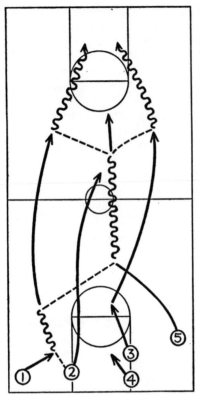

Chart 16. We keep considerable defensive strength at the opponents' free-throw area. No. 2 will tip back to No. 1. No. 4 and No. 3 will tip to No. 5, who is out a little more. If No. 2 tips to No. 1, he will immediately start a dribble, looking for No. 5 or No. 3 cutting for the middle. If he can get the ball out to No. 5, then No. 5 will straighten out and go down the middle with a dribble, and No. 3 will cut behind him. If No. 3 gets the pass, No. 5 will stay on the right-hand side of the floor. No. 5 will go all the way if he can, or he will feed No. 3 or No. 1. No. 2 is a trailer and No. 4 is the safety defensive man.

passing off, always alert and ready to break for the basket. The passes are short and fast. The players all watch the man with the ball and if an opportunity occurs, they cut for the basket whether they have the ball or not. It is a crisscross and weaving pattern using well all the pivots, reverses and feints of the game. Very little dribbling is employed. Speed and deception are essential. This is a very effective style of play and when a team employing it has a good lead going into the closing minutes of the game, it is almost impossible to take the ball away from them, because they move it so rapidly.

Fast break

This is also an effective offense that can be used against a defense that picks up all over the floor. The same weaving method is employed to advance the ball over the center line and it is rare

FAST BREAK AFTER SUCCESSFUL FREE THROW

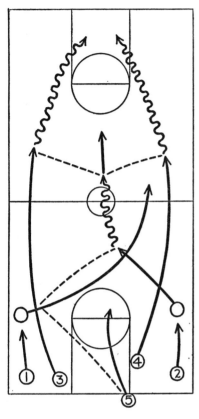

Chart 17. No. 3 taps the ball to No. 5, who has jumped out in order to get the ball in quickly for a fast break. We prefer to throw to No. 2 if possible; but in this case, let us assume that he is covered. No. 1 and No. 2 start as soon as they see the free throw has been made. No. 5 will then pass to No. 1. No. 2 will break for the center of the floor and Nos. 3 and 4 will cut in the lines indicated. No. 1 will pass to No. 2, who will dribble as far as he can and then pass to No. 3 or No. 4. No. 1 will be the trailer and No. 5 the safety defensive man.

indeed that a team well drilled in this "give and go" system of play is ever prevented from bringing the ball over the center line.

Hints for offensive teams

1. Keep the center open.
2. Pass accurately.
3. Look first.
4. Go to meet the ball.
5. Don't pass to the sideline.
6. Keep out of the corners.
7. Clear space for teammates.
8. Screen for teammates.
9. Don't shoot unless you have a perfect setup for a follow-up.
10. Control the ball.

15

Offensive Guard Play

In modern basketball it is highly essential that all of the men on the team be scoring threats. Today you will find that the guards who are essentially defensive men generally do as much scoring as the forwards.

The guard play in basketball, or the guard-around play as we call it here, has been much discussed in many coaching schools. In fact, our guard-around play is so designed that we consider it the best fundamental ball handling drill we have found. As can be seen from the diagrams, the setup is the same in every case with six options for the guard to exercise as he sees fit. We have shown this guard-around play at many coaching schools and, in every case, it has caused considerable comment by the coaches. The reason for this, we think, is due to the fact that we spend a lot of time on it and, therefore, in our demonstrations it looks better than the other things we attempt to show. Here are a few pointers to help coaches in developing this play.

1. A guard must be an excellent ball handler.
2. A guard must have speed.
3. All guard-around plays must be run with maximum speed in ball handling and in footwork.
4. A guard should in every case be playing on his toes, his knees bent, his hips down, and his head up; in other words, in a driving position.
5. The guard is the quarterback of his team and must not start a play unless there is reasonable assurance that it will go through to a swift conclusion.
6. The guard-around play will work best when the guard is over near the sideline.
7. A guard should cut right off the tail of the forward in a straight line at the basket. Again, don't run in circles. The charts with the explanations will show briefly how the plays are executed.

GUARD-AROUND PLAYS

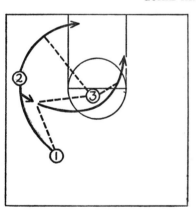

Chart 18. PLAY 1: Guard No. 1 passes to Forward No. 2, who steps out to meet the pass. He immediately throws the ball to No. 3, the pivot man, and cuts around him. Guard No. 1 goes in with his pass and No. 3 passes either to him or to No. 2.

This series of guard plays takes care of every type of defense. Regardless of how a defensive man maneuvers, one of these plays is designed to meet the situation.

From these setups the Kentucky offense is built. It can clearly

GUARD-AROUND PLAYS (Cont.)

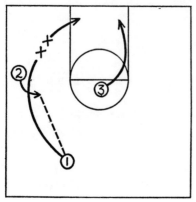

Chart 19. PLAY 2: Guard No. 1 passes to Forward No. 2, who steps out to meet the pass in every case and turns his body as if to pass to No. 3. But as he turns he flips the ball to the guard who is cutting by, and the guard takes one dribble and shoots.

Chart 20. PLAY 3: Guard No. 1 passes to No. 2, who turns toward the center of the floor, takes one dribble, jumps in the air, and hooks a pass to the guard who has cut by.

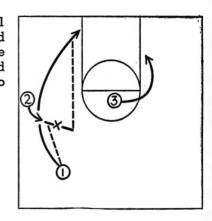

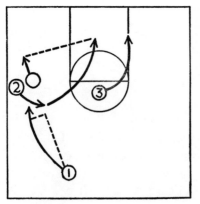

Chart 21. PLAY 4: No. 1 passes to No. 2, who flips ball to No. 1 as in PLAY 2. But No. 1 jumps in the air and hooks the pass to No. 2.

GUARD-AROUND PLAYS (Cont.)

Chart 22. PLAY 5: Guard No. 1 passes to No. 2, who takes one dribble, pivots, and passes back to No. 1.

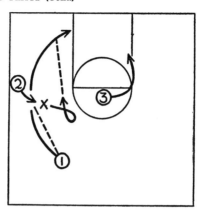

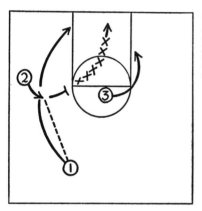

Chart 23. PLAY 6: Guard No. 1 passes to No. 2, who takes ball, fakes as if to pass to Guard No. 1, but keeps the ball and dribbles in to shoot.

Chart 24. PLAY 7: This is known as an inside screen. No. 1 passes to No. 2, and No. 2 makes his pass to No. 3 before No. 1 arrives for the screen. No. 1 screens the defense man on No. 2; and then, after No. 2 cuts in the direction indicated on the chart, No. 1 cuts for the basket and receives a pass from No. 3, if open.

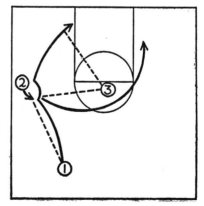

GUARD-AROUND PLAYS (Cont.)

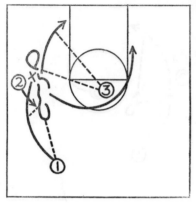

Chart 25. PLAY 8: In this play, No. 1 passes to No. 2 and No. 2 flips the ball to No. 1, the same as in PLAY 2. No. 1 takes one dribble, pivots to the outside, and passes to No. 3. No. 2, in the meantime, goes out two steps, fakes to the inside toward No. 3, and then pivots and cuts directly behind No. 1, using him as a screen. No. 3 passes to No. 2, if open; but, if the defensive man on No. 1 shifts to take No. 2, then the pass is given to No. 1 as indicated on the chart.

Chart 26. PLAY 9: Here No. 1 passes to No. 2 and goes to his outside. No. 2 flips pass to No. 1. No. 1 takes one dribble, pivots to outside, and passes to No. 3. No. 2, in the meantime, goes out two steps, fakes to the inside toward No. 3, then goes to the inside of No. 1 and establishes an inside screen. No 1 cuts right off of No. 2, and No. 3 gives pass to the one that is open.

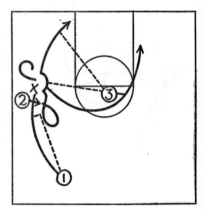

be seen that we depend a great deal on our defensive men being equally as good scoring threats as our centers and forwards. In other words, we feel here that by clever ball handling, two boys can set up a very well defined offense. When they have exhausted the possibilities of two men playing together they invite the third man or pivot man into the play and the possibilities that have been charted are used. These plays can be used on both sides of the floor and are excellent ball handling drills to be used as fundamental setups. We go through these in practice almost every day and therefore, not only develop excellent ball handling, change of direction, goal shooting, and other necessary details but at the same time we build up our complete offense.

OTHER PLAYS OFF THE PIVOT

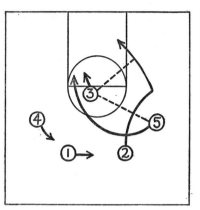

Chart 27. No. 2 passes to No. 5 and cuts on the inside of the receiver to screen his man. No. 5 passes to No. 3 and both No. 2 and No. 5 cut for basket. No. 3 passes to free man.

Chart 28. The play starts in the same way, with No. 2 passing to No. 5. This time, however, No. 2 goes down outside, using No. 5 as a screen. The latter passes to No. 3 and cuts for basket. No. 3 feeds the free man.

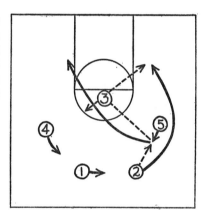

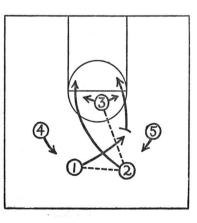

Chart 29. No. 1 passes to No. 2 and sets up a screen for him. No. 2 passes to No. 3, and both he and No. 1 cut for basket. The ball goes to the free man.

OTHER PLAYS OFF THE PIVOT (Cont.)

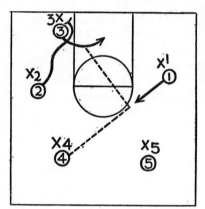

Chart 30. No. 4 passes to No. 1, who cuts to meet pass. No. 2 cuts to screen for No. 3, who swings around screen and takes pass from No. 1.

Chart 31. No. 1 passes to pivot No. 4, who fakes to No. 5 going around but passes to No. 2, who delays for about two counts after No. 1 has passed to No. 4. No. 2 dribbles in to the basket or passes to No. 3. No. 4 should be a good follow man, No. 2 a quick starter, fast, and a good long shot.

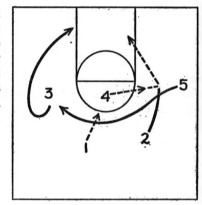

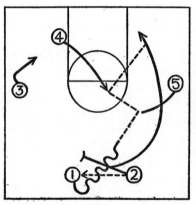

Chart 32. No. 2 passes to No. 1 and screens for him. No. 1 dribbles past him and passes to No. 5, who has come to meet the pass. No. 4 has cut out to the pivot position. No. 1 cuts behind No. 5 on guard-around play and receives pass from No. 4. No. 3 goes in for rebound and No. 2 stays back for defense.

OTHER PLAYS OFF THE PIVOT (Cont.)

Chart 33. No. 2 passes to No. 1 and goes over and screens for him. No. 1 passes in to the pivot man, No. 4, and cuts for the basket. No. 5 times his movements so that he creates a second screen for No. 1. No. 4 gives the ball to No. 1, who dribbles on in for a score.

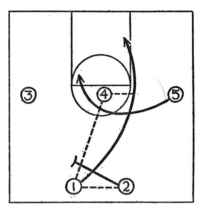

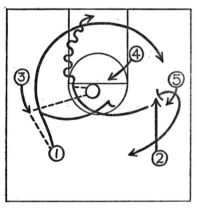

Chart 34. No. 1 passes to No. 3, who comes out to meet the pass. No. 1 cuts in fast as in the other plays. No. 2 starts at the same time as No. 1 and screens for No. 5. No. 5 cuts right behind No. 2 and then around the pivot man, No. 4. No. 4 has come out to meet the pass from No. 3. No. 3 screens again for No. 5, and No. 4 hands No. 5 the ball as he goes by. No. 5 takes one dribble and shoots. No. 2 comes back out for defensive assignment.

Chart 35. No. 1 passes to No. 3 and cuts past him, but not so deep as usual. No. 5 sets a back screen on the defensive man who is on No. 2. No. 4 comes out to meet the pass from No. 3. No. 4 feeds the ball to No. 2, if open. If defensive man on No. 5 shifts to pick up No. 2, No. 5 has inside position and cuts in line shown and gets the ball. No. 3 comes out for safety position.

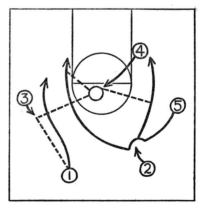

OTHER PLAYS OFF THE PIVOT (Cont.)

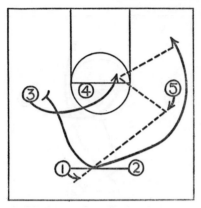

Chart 36. No. 2 passes to No. 1 and cuts by him, creating a brush screen, but continues on to screen for No. 3. No. 1 passes to No. 5, who comes out to meet the pass. No. 5 passes to No. 3, who is cutting for the basket. If No. 3 isn't open, No. 1 has continued on and behind No. 5 and may get a pass from No. 3. No. 4 pulls to make room for the play.

THREE OUT—TWO IN OFFENSIVE PLAYS

Chart 37. No. 3 passes to No. 2 and cuts hard to line shown. If he can run by his defensive man, No. 2 may give him a pass. If not, then pass is made to No. 5, who is coming out to meet the pass. No. 3 has continued his cut and goes over and screens for No. 4, who, in turn, receives a pass from No. 5. No. 5 then cuts for the basket and may get a flip pass back, if No. 4 is unable to shoot.

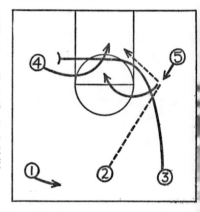

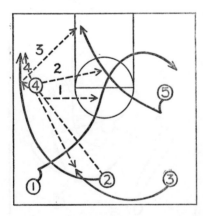

Chart 38. In this play No. 4 and No. 5 are set up somewhat farther from the back line. (1) No. 2 passes to No. 4 and screens for No. 1, who cuts for the basket. No. 4 tries to pass to No. 1, if No. 1 is open. (2) If the option is not present, No. 5 times his movement to cut off of No. 1, and No. 4 tries to pass to No. 5. (3) If he cannot get a good pass to No. 5 on his cut, No. 4 may pivot and give the ball to No. 5 as he tries for position under the basket. (4)

Or he may give it to No. 2, who has cut behind No. 4. If all options are closed, No. 4 passes out to No. 3. (The passes are numbered on the chart in the sequence of the options.)

THREE OUT—TWO IN OFFENSIVE PLAYS (Cont.)

Chart 39. No. 3 passes to No. 2 and screens for him as No. 2 dribbles behind him and passes to No. 5. No. 3 goes on and screens for No. 1, who uses a terrific burst of speed down the middle. No. 5 passes to No. 1, who dribbles in, uses a jump shot, or passes to No. 4. No. 5 cuts in for the rebound. No. 3 stays back for defense.

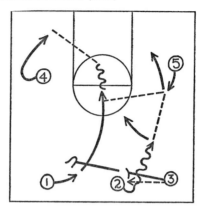

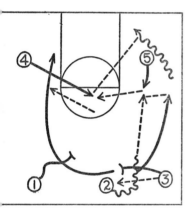

Chart 40. No. 3 passes to No. 2 and screens for him as No. 2 dribbles behind him and passes to No. 5. No. 2 continues, and No. 5 will give him a pass, if he is open, and No. 2 will dribble in for basket. If No. 2 is not open, No. 5 will pass to No. 4, who has cut to the pivot. No. 3 continues his move, and No. 1 screens for him. No. 3 cuts for the basket, and No. 4 passes to him. There is also the option of passing to No. 2. No. 1 stays back for defense.

Chart 41. No. 2 starts the play by passing to No. 1. As No. 2 passes he cuts for the basket and then swings back to screen off the defensive man on No. 3. No. 1 passes to No. 4, who comes out to meet pass. No. 4 passes to No. 3, who is cutting down the middle of the floor. No. 2 stays for defense. Nos. 4 and 5 will follow for rebound.

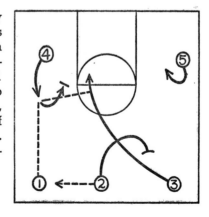

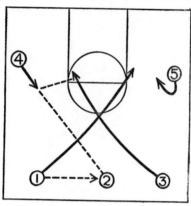

Chart 42. No. 1 passes to No.
and, as he does so, he cuts in th
path indicated. No. 2 passes t
No. 4, who comes out to meet th
pass. As in all plays, the ma:
who does not have the ball mus
do the timing. No. 3 then time
his cut, cutting behind No. 1, an
No. 4 gives him the pass. No.
stays for defense.

Chart 43. No. 1 passes to No. 4,
who comes out to meet the pass.
No. 5 cuts for the pivot position,
and, as he comes out, No. 4
passes to him. No. 1 cuts behind
No. 4, and No. 5 gives him the
pass, if open. Otherwise, he gives
it to No. 4, who cuts in line shown
on chart. No. 2 screens for No.
3, and, if both No. 1 and No. 4 are
covered, then No. 5 may give the
ball to No. 3 for a medium shot.
No. 2 stays back for defense.

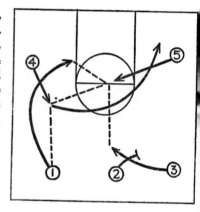

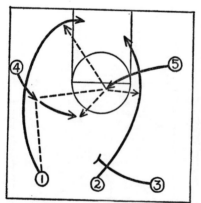

Chart 44. No. 1 passes to No. 4,
who comes to meet the pass. No.
5 cuts for the pivot, and, as he
does, No. 4 gives him a pass. No.
3 screens for No. 2, and No. 2
cuts for the basket. No. 5 will give
the ball to No. 1 or to No. 2. If
both are covered, he may give it
to No. 4 for a medium shot. No. 3
stays back for defense.

THREE OUT—TWO IN OFFENSIVE PLAYS (Cont.)

Chart 45. No. 2 passes to No. 3 and, as he does so, he goes to screen for No. 3. No. 3 passes in to No. 5, who comes out to meet the pass. No. 3 cuts for the basket and No. 5 gives him the ball. No. 1 stays back for defense. No. 4 times his movement to go in for rebound.

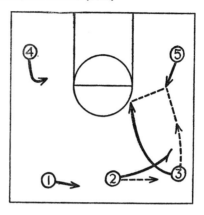

Chart 46. No. 2 passes to No. 1 and goes over to screen for him, but continues a step or so. No. 1 dribbles down the middle. He stops and passes to No. 4. No. 2 so times his move that he runs his guard into No. 1 and keeps on going down the middle to take a pass from No. 4. No. 3 stays back for defense.

OUT-OF-BOUNDS PLAYS

Chart 47. No. 3 tries for the inside position on defensive man X2. Just as he cuts for this position, No. 2 cuts behind him, and for the basket. If X3 follows No. 3, then No. 2 is open. If X3 shifts and takes No. 2, then No. 3 should be open, for he has established an inside position on X2 and should have an open path to the basket. No. 1 will pass to whichever man is open.

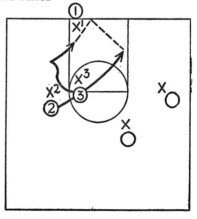

OUT-OF-BOUNDS PLAYS (Cont.)

Chart 48. The formation is balanced to the side of the floor where the ball is taken out of bounds in order to get a better pass in position. No. 3 tries for an inside screen on X2. No. 2 cuts right behind him. If X3 follows No. 3, then No. 2 is open for the pass from No. 4. If X3 shifts to take No. 2, then No. 1 will be open, for he is cutting right off No. 3 and X2 and X1 are screened

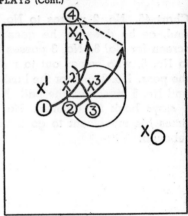

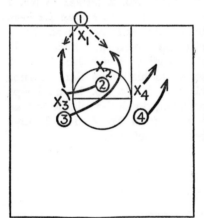

Chart 49. No. 2 lines up for back screen. In this case he screens for No. 3 by slipping up from behind. No. 3 cuts for the basket; if X2 follows No. 2 out, then No. 3 will be open for the pass from No. 1. If X2 shifts to take No. 3, then No. 2 will be open, because he has an inside position on No. 3 and a clear path to the basket.

Chart 50. This is exactly the same setup as above, only in this case No. 2 just keeps on going. X2, expecting the same play as above, plans to shift as No. 4 cuts down the middle. No. 2 doesn't screen but turns and goes back to the basket. A screen was expected and none occurred.

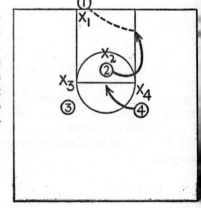

1. Player is crouched. Ball
been drawn back near right
opposite foot forward. Right
is bent, left arm at right
es to it.

Plate 2. Ball has been released with a wrist snap,
arms extended, thumbs
pointing upward and out.
(Wallace Jones)

ONE-HANDED
UNDERHAND
PASS

Plate 3. Player is crouched
like a bowler. Front hand
guides, other hand behind
the ball; wrists bent down,
thumbs out.

Plate 4. Front hand has been taken off the ball, back hand behind the ball; weight flowing to the front foot.

Plate 6. Ball is held above head, arms fully extended, hands covering sides and rear of ball, thumbs behind.

Plate 5. Complete follow-through; palm facing upward; weight on front foot, as player swings into play. (Kenneth Rollins)

Plate 7. Ball has been released with a wrist snap. Weight is on toes ready to shift into play. (Wallace Jones)

TWO-HANDED
OVERHEAD
PASS

Plate 8.

Plate 9.

ONE-HANDED OVERHEAD PASS (VERNON HATTON)

Plate 10.

Plate 11.

Plate 12. Player is in crouched ~~position~~ tion ready to pass the ball in ~~bounds~~ out of bounds.

ONE-HANDED ROLL PASS

Plate 13. He drops his body, and the arm with the ball, the ball near the floor. He looks for teammate.

Plate 14. He quickly turns hea~~d~~ original position to draw defe~~nse~~ man's hand down, opposite han~~d~~ and then by wrist snap rolls the ~~ball~~ to teammate. (Cliff Barker, left~~)~~

Plate 15. Offensive player fakes ball upward to draw defensive man up. (Cliff Barker with ball, Wallace Jones, right)

Plate 16. Offensive man brings the ball down and cups the ball with hand and wrist. Second man starts to move into the play, ready for pass.

Plate 17. His body weight is lowered as he flips ball with wrist action to teammate breaking for basket. Notice position of hands and head.

BACKHAND PASS (Cont.)

Plate 18. Offensive man straightens out and shifts for rebound. Notice position of head, arms, and hand of man shooting lay-up shot.

Plate 19. In the two-handed push shot the ball is thrown toward the basket with a push of the ball as the arms are extended and the knees straight. This picture is an excellent illustration of the ball as it leaves the hands, arms fully extended, player finishing on his toes, ready to follow the shot. (Gayle Rose)

**TWO-HANDED
UNDERHAND
SHOT**

Plate 20. One foot is slightly back of the other. Hands are on the side of the ball. The ball is held by the fingers.

Plate 21. As shot is attempted, body is lowered, knees bent. Ball is brought down between legs, wrists bent; eyes on basket.

Plate 22. The ball is lifted into the basket. Player finishes the throw with complete follow-through. (Cliff Barker)

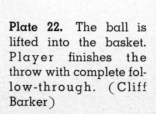

**TWO-HANDED
OVERHEAD
SHOT**

Plate 23. Ball is held directly overhead with arms fully extended.

Plate 24. As shot is attempted, the knees and arms bend slightly to give leverage to the shot, eyes on the basket.

Plate 25. Shooter finishes by straightening body, arms fully extended, hands facing the basket. (Wallace Jones)

ONE-HANDED TURN-AROUND SHOT
(BURROW SHOOTING, BECK GUARDING)

Plate 26. Feet are parallel, knees bent, ball held out in front. Fake is made with ball, head, and body.

Plate 27. Ball is held higher to make defensive man commit to guard ball.

Plate 28. In shooting with the left hand the step is started with the right foot to gain a good take-off position.

ONE-HANDED
TURN-AROUND SHOT
(Cont.)

Plate 29. Foot has been planted and body has continued to turn with weight on right foot for beginning of jump. Eyes on basket, body between ball and defensive man.

Plate 30. Turn has almost been completed. Ball is held away from defensive man at beginning of jump.

Plate 31. Perfect illustration of the one-handed turn-around shot as it is completed. Body is turned toward basket, arm fully extended, player in excellent position for rebounding.

Plate 32. If attempted by the right hand, the right foot is forward, knees slightly bent. The left hand is below the ball.

Plate 33. Ball is brought up near the face, arms bent, left hand slightly in front and below, right hand behind ball.

Plate 34. Right arm is straightened as ball is thrown toward basket. Left hand acts as guide. (Cliff Barker)

Plate 35. This shot is attempted near the basket, and usually by pivot men. The ball is held directly in front.

Plate 36. If attempted with the right hand, the player will face to the right. Body crouched to get leg spring.

ONE-HANDED FLIP SHOT

Plate 37. The right leg is used for take-off, the ball is brought up high over the head as the body turns to the right.

Plate 38. As the shot is completed the right arm will be completely extended, the hand facing the basket. (Wallace Jones)

Plate 39. This picture illustrates rebounding under an offensive board. Burrow is player No. 50. He has leaped in the air, has his hand above the basket, and has tipped the ball into the basket. This shows an excellent form with both arms fully extended.

Plate 40. This illustrates the jump shot. Burrow has leaped into the air with both hands on the ball. His right hand is behind the ball, his left hand is used as guide. As he attains his maximum height he will release the ball, pushing it to the basket.

RIGHT ONE-HANDED
PIVOT SHOT

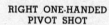

Plate 41. This illustrates excellent form in the right one-handed pivot shot.

LEFT ONE-HANDED
PIVOT SHOT

Plate 42. This shows the same player executing the same shot with his left hand. Pivot men today must be able to shoot well with either hand. This and Plate 41 show excellent form in the same individual.

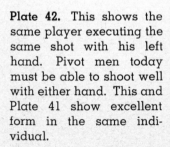

SIDE OUT-OF-BOUNDS PLAY

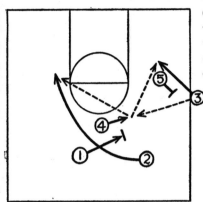

Chart 51. No. 3 passes to No. 4, who comes in to meet ball. Meanwhile, No. 5 screens for No. 3 and No. 1 for No. 2. Either No. 3 or No. 2 gets pass from No. 4.

OUT-OF-BOUNDS, UNDER-BASKET PLAY

Chart 52. No. 2 screens for No. 1 and No. 3 for No. 4. At signal from No. 5, No. 1 and No. 4 break for basket, No. 5 passing to free man.

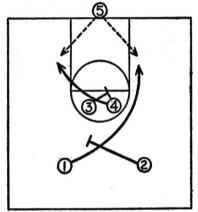

CENTER TIP-OFF PLAYS

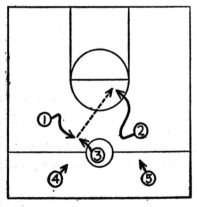

Chart 53. No. 1 fakes toward the basket and then comes back to take tap slightly to the side but in front of the circle. No. 2 fakes in for tap but pivots and cuts for the basket. No. 1 passes to No. 2.

Chart 54. No. 1 feints toward the basket, then cuts back to take tap at the side of the circle. He bats ball to No. 4, who is cutting for the basket. No. 4 dribbles in for a basket or, if guarded, may pass to No. 2.

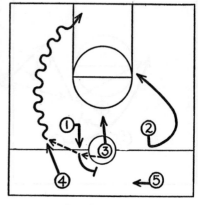

PLAYS AGAINST THE ZONE DEFENSE

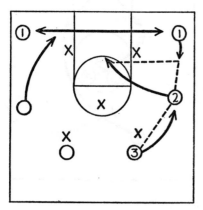

Chart 55. This is a diagram of what I have found to be a very effective method in working against a zone defense. No. 1, center, floats from one side to the other as shown. Play works on either side. No. 3 passes to No. 2. No. 2 passes immediately to No. 1 and then cuts to basket for a return pass. If No. 1 cannot pass to No. 2, he passes to No. 3, who has cut to the spot vacated by No. 2. He shoots or passes to No. 1 and cuts for the basket. This chart I think will give you the most difficult defense to penetrate owing to the fact that it is the 2-1-2 defense. (See X's on chart.) Naturally, if you are playing against a 3-2 zone, this play would work even better. You will also note that, when No. 2 cuts for the basket, he will be on the inside of all the defensive players. The pass from No. 1 to him should not be difficult. The important things to remember are that the passes should be well timed, that they should be made quickly and accurately, and that the cutting should be at top speed. The important things about attacking every zone defense are to move the ball quickly and to cut for the basket. As I have said on many occasions before, there is no defense against good ball handling.

PLAYS AGAINST THE ZONE DEFENSE (Cont.)

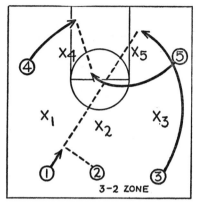

Chart 56. This play works well against the 3-2 zone defense. No. 1 cuts inside X1. No. 2 gives No. 1 a pass and, just as the pass begins, No. 5 cuts for the basket near the free-throw line. No. 1 passes to No. 5. No. 4 cuts behind X4, and No. 3 cuts around behind X5. No. 5 can shoot, or pass to No. 4 or No. 3.

Chart 57. No. 2 passes to No. 3. No. 3 passes in to No. 5 and continues to cut around behind him and behind X5. No. 4 cuts for the free-throw line, and No. 5 passes to him. No. 4 shoots, or passes to No. 1 or No. 3.

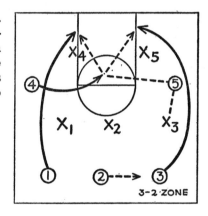

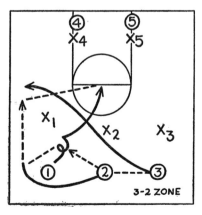

Chart 58. No. 3 passes to No. 2 and cuts in the line indicated. No. 1 takes the inside position on X1. No. 2 passes to No. 1 and cuts around behind him. No. 1 flips the ball to No. 2, who immediately passes in to No. 3, who has now arrived at spot near the sideline. No. 3 takes a shot from here or passes in to No. 1, who has timed his cut for the basket. No. 4 and No. 5 stay near the basket to keep X4 and X5 back with them.

PLAYS AGAINST THE ZONE DEFENSE (Cont.)

Chart 59. No. 5 moves from side to side. When he reaches one of the corners, the play begins and goes to the side that he is on. No. 2 passes to No. 4. No. 3 cuts for the free-throw line and gets pass from No. 4. No. 1 cuts behind Nos. 3 and 4. No. 5 times his cut, and No. 4 does also. If all men move as indicated, No. 3 can shoot or pass to No. 1, to No. 5, or back to No. 4.

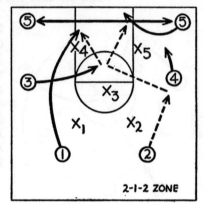

2-1-2 ZONE

16

Kentucky's Continuity Offense

Basketball continuites are used most successfully by teams with a slow set style of game. However, some fast-break teams make good use of a continuity when they fail to get the desired situation for a shot at the goal. There are many different continuous-action plays but the accompanying diagrams (Charts 60 and 61) explain only the one we use.

Continuity plays are very effective especially in the sections where close screening is permitted. There are three-man continuities and five-man continuities. They need not necessarily be as exact as the one that is diagrammed here because the freedom style of offense that is taught by some coaches is really a continuous movement and therefore may be considered a continuity.

Our most successful continuity is our figure eight with its variations. This play is very valuable to any coach as a fundamental drill, as an offensive play, or as a stall game or possession game. The drill gives the boys stamina and endurance and helps teach the lay-up shot when going in with the greatest speed.

Charts 60 and 61

This five-man figure eight, showing three men out and two in, gives a team a good pass and cut game with an equal distribution of the five players over the front court leaving the middle lane to the goal open for the cutting.

It is possible to run this continuity and instantly go to our pattern from which we are confident we can score. Making this play occasionally during a game has a tendency to loosen up a defense by changing our offensive assignments. We have three boys who can play the pivot position; therefore, by running this continuity we can switch our players and bring any of these three to the pivot. This may cross up the opponents' defense.

The movement starts when our team has tried a fast break and has failed to get the shot, or when it has brought the ball down slowly and got set in our positions as in Chart 60A. The ball moves to the player cutting from the sideline and the passer cutting for the goal. If the passer gets open he should be given a lead pass as he goes to the corner of the front court on the opposite side of the court that he cuts from, as in Chart 60B. Player 4 passes to 5 who meets the pass. No. 4 cuts for the goal and, if open, receives lead pass from 5. If 4 does not get open he goes to the right corner. Player 5 now passes the ball to 3 and cuts for the goal. If 5 does not receive pass, he cuts to corner as is shown in Chart 60C. The play continues as is shown through Charts 60 and 61.

Should your opponents play away from you, good medium length shots may be taken, or if they use a "pressure" defense the short shots should be gotten. This play is very good if you have a lead going into the last stages of the ball game. It is a good stall play and will make the zone defense come out and play man for man if they get a chance at the ball. When each player has played

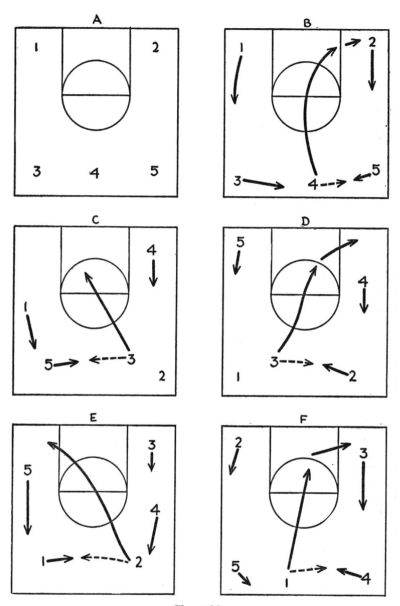

Chart 60.

each spot and moved as he should, the action has gone through a figure eight movement. In Chart 61F it will be shown how easy it is to set up a pivot post offense from this variation, and that is our basic formation.

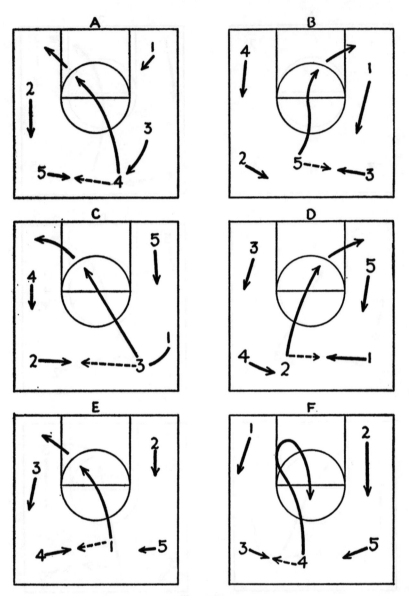

Chart 61.

17

Individual Defense

The defensive philosophy here at the University of Kentucky is aggressive rather than passive. We attempt to take the initiative away from the offense by applying pressure on every offensive man, rather than passively countering the offensive moves. We want to guard our opponents so closely that the man with the ball has difficulty passing or dribbling—and, above all, difficulty in shooting.

It naturally follows that, if we make it difficult for our opponents to receive passes, we cause them to make mistakes, like bad passes, walking and double-dribbling violations, and poor shots.

This kind of defense puts pressure on the opponent with the ball from all five of our defensive men, rather than from just the individual who is guarding him.

The most important feature of individual defensive play, I would say, would be never to allow a man to get between you and the basket. Regardless of the position that the offensive man takes on the floor, the defensive man must take a position that will prevent the offensive man from having a direct path to the basket. In offense, we teach our players to outmaneuver, to get a step on the defensive man. So, in defensive play, the opposite should be in order. If the offensive man is at a distance from the basket, the guard as a rule will not play him as closely as when he is close in. Some men must be played closer than others but a general rule would be to play a man near enough so that he can be adequately guarded but not so close that he will be allowed to break by for a chance to score.

In playing under or near the basket, watch to see that the offensive man does not get position on you by making you stay behind him. If the offensive man moves near the basket be sure that he does not push under the basket and then line directly in front where he can receive a pass, pivot, and score. In this particular case, it may be necessary for you to play in front of him or at least well around to his side to prevent him from getting what is called "position."

A guard should always keep his eyes on the ball and on the men at the same time. I said "men" because one man is not enough. In the game as played today, a lot of screening takes place. If you are not careful, and watch only your man a screen may be created and you will be boxed. Therefore, watch all the men who move in your direction because you must learn to "switch" if screened in order to cooperate with your teammates.

A defensive man should force an opponent to take long, hurried shots. If you can force a team to take long shots, the chances of their hitting the basket are not very great. If you can make them hurry these shots as well, the accuracy of their shooting will further diminish.

In order to prevent fouling, a good rule to follow is: Play the ball and not the man. A clever ball handler can make a guard foul him. As I have said before, study your man, catalog his weaknesses and strengths and try to out-guess him. If you can prevent him from getting a pass, play him accordingly.

A guard must always maintain an inside position. This holds

true on play from center. If an opponent is dribbling, maintain an inside position and drive him to the side-lines. Don't stand flat-footed and slap at the ball. Get in motion with the man, use your inside hand and try to take the ball away in that fashion. Be careful that he does not stop quickly, throw you off balance, and then take a quick shot at the basket. As a defensive player, being caught flat-footed or off balance is one of the greatest mistakes you can make.

Another grave error is to take your eyes off a man after he passes. Nine times out of ten the best pass is a return pass to this man. After a man passes, all eyes generally follow the ball. You must watch this passer so that he does not take advantage of this and make a quick break for the basket. Stay with this man after he passes.

In rebound work under the defensive basket we tell our boys never to bat the ball. The danger here lies in the fact that they may bat it to an opponent and allow him to score. The rule that we follow is to catch all balls coming off the backboard and to pass out as quickly as possible and as far as possible. Since we depend on a quick break on offense the long pass cuts off the opponents. A guard must start the offense quickly and must learn to get the ball out fast or the fast break system will not prove successful.

The footwork of a guard is important. We have mentioned elsewhere that we study our footwork so that our position is proper anywhere on the floor. A guard should slide with an opponent and not cross-step or cross his feet. He should play on his toes and in a crouched position. He should have a stance that is comfortable and that will enable him to drive quickly in any direction. He should keep his arms outstretched, swinging up and down to harass the opponent in shooting and passing, and to cover as much territory as possible in order to block passes. This slows up the offense for it prevents the man with the ball from making many passes that he would otherwise attempt. A guard must be careful not to play too far under the basket or the opponents, in rebounding, will drive the guard out of bounds. After a guard gains possession of the ball he should get it out of the danger zone immediately. He should not dribble in the back court if he can pass out.

A guard should not charge an opponent. He should always approach the offensive player with feet apart in order to be able to shift to meet the offensive man's tactics. If he should charge the offensive player, the latter will side-step and make a break for the basket. A defensive player should watch his opponent's footwork and body balance; if the offensive player makes mistakes, the defensive player should profit accordingly. Along this same line, we might add that a defensive man should not jump in the air at the man who has possession of the ball because it will allow the opponent to side-step him and get by for a clear shot at the basket. As a general rule, I would say: Never jump in the air to block a shot. If the man with the ball bluffs a shot, then the guard off his feet is out of the play. It is best to keep one's balance at all times. However, a leap for a positive shot may be attempted as a gamble.

If it is apparent that a man in dribbling down will take off for a shot, a defensive man rushing in certainly must leave his feet to block the shot. After watching games in the N.C.A.A. and Olympic Tournaments which brought together some of the finest athletes in the nation, I would say that there were numerous occasions during the play in which the guards positively prevented baskets by leaving their feet and knocking balls away that were certainly headed for the scorebook.

Another fundamental of good guarding is that if a guard is caught alone with two opponents, he should never allow either of them to draw him away from the vicinity of the basket. Force the shot from as great a distance as possible. Only after a shot has been taken do you stop playing your man. Turn, block him out, and take the ball off the backboard.

A guard should never go down on a play unless there is someone covering his territory. One guard should always remain in a defensive position. With that, let me add that a guard should not be content to be a guard only. Develop your basket-shooting eye. Good goal-scoring guards are at a premium. If your team is getting the tip-off, have a guard go down on scoring plays. But, remember, a guard must also watch for the opposing guard to crash through on tip-off plays. In this case the guards must be prepared to pick them up. Let me add again, for the sake of safety: Keep an inside position and never allow an opponent to get behind you.

Remember, all players on the team are guards when the opponents have the ball. After your team has taken a shot, stay and fight for the ball. Do not surrender it without a fight by dropping back on defense immediately after the shot has been attempted.

You are never too late on defense. When everything looks hopeless that is the time to dig in. Many times a pass will be intercepted and one of your opponents will be driving for the basket. Go after him. Get in a good position for the rebound because there is a reasonable chance that he will miss it. Many times I have seen a defensive man quit, the basket missed, and another one of the opponents come down and tap in the ball when all the defensive man had to do was to dig in and get down there himself. At other times I have seen one defensive man down fighting against two offensive men who are trying to tip in a basket. Another defensive player should hurry down and help. You are never too late in this case. A step or two may prevent the basket and at the same time, prevent a defeat.

Put the heat on an offensive man. Too many guards allow an offensive man an opportunity to catch a pass and then move up and try to guard that man. Our guarding demands that you put the pressure on an offensive man and prevent him from catching the pass. Remember this: if you allow a team to handle the ball, they will beat you. Keep an aggressive, stubborn defense on your man.

Again, in a pick-up defense keep the pressure on and be sure that it is not your man who will be freed for a pass. There is no use in having a pick-up defense if one player is not picking up tightly.

When two players drive down against you, try to make them commit themselves. Jump at the man with the ball, slap your feet to try to stop them; yell at them. Your teammates are on the way to help you. It may take only a second for their arrival.

If you are playing against a screening offense and you are being screened, then take the screener. Talk with your teammates and tell them what you are doing.

Every player on the team is a guard when the opponents have the ball, and the two primary duties are: first, to take the ball away from the opponents, and secondly, to prevent a shot. Take pride in your defense. It is hard work and it is not spectacular. If you have the proper attitude in regard to this, it will influence your team play. Your men may not be spectacular shooters; they may have to earn their glory by being great defensive men and preventing the opponents' outstanding men from scoring. Again, there is sufficient glory in victory for everyone.

Other defensive hints

1. *Stance.* Use a boxer's stance with the feet well under and not too widely spread, the hips down, on the toes, knees bent, back straight, head up, arms in close. Keep the eyes on the opponent and watch the other men breaking by.

2. *Footwork.* Take short steps and do not cross step but slide your feet. Do not rush; go cautiously. In guarding against a dribbler go with him using your inside hand and do not stab.

3. *Mental guarding.* Anticipate movements. Anticipate passes. Talk to your opponent. Remember you are at a disadvantage because you must second-guess his movements.

4. *Guarding man without the ball.*
   TIP-OFF: Have an inside position. Fight for the ball and be sure you do not get trapped with a quick slap pass to an opponent cutting behind you.
   SET PLAYS: On set plays, play tight remembering that the defense occurs on a man before he catches the ball and not afterward. If the play is on the opposite side of the floor you may loosen up but keep your eyes on your opponent.
   OUT-OF-BOUNDS PLAYS: Anticipate the movements and be sure that you will not be screened. Many of these plays can be solved as soon as they are set up. Talk to your teammates if you anticipate these movements.
   POSITION OF GUARDS: In guarding a man near the sidelines be sure to maintain a position that will not give him a direct path to the basket. In guarding a man near the basket assume a position that will prevent him from getting a pass.
   DEFENSE FOR SCREENERS: Switch. If a man screens you, take the screener. Talk and tell your teammate to switch.

5. *Guarding man with the ball.* If out on the floor, the speed

of the opponent will determine how you must play him. If he is a good long shot you must play him close. If he is not a good shot but fast, then stay away from him at such a distance that he cannot drive past you. Watch the position of the feet of your opponent. If near the basket, be careful where you place your feet in guarding him so that he cannot step to the side of and around you by wrapping your leg with his. Watch for feints and do not go for them. If possible, anticipate his movements but make him commit himself. Watch for men who may be cutting in to screen for your opponent. Watch him after he passes and do not take your eyes off him.

6. *Preventing opponent from dribbling around.* Our first step in countering an opponent's fake or move is to retreat with the rear foot. If the opponent is moving to our right, then our second step is also with the right foot, if that is our rear foot. If he moves to our left and our right foot is the rear foot, then the second step is with the left or forward foot. Get into position before guarding or attempting to play the ball.

7. *Breaking up the dribble.*
   A. The guard must move with short, chopping steps. Get in motion. Do not stand and reach.
   B. The guard should run in a crouched position with the head below the armpit of the dribbler.
   C. Be one-half step ahead of the dribbler.
   D. If the guard cannot deflect or intercept the ball, he must get into position between the dribbler and the goal.
   E. Striking the ball:
      (1) If the guard is not quick enough to intercept the ball, he should attempt to slap the ball with the hand farthest from the dribbler.
   F. Stealing the ball:
      (1) If the guard is quick, he should get in as close to the dribbler as possible and have the hand nearest the dribbler come up under the dribbler's arms as he steals the ball.

8. *Blocking the lay-up shot at the end of the dribble.* Use the hand nearest the basket, or the ball, in blocking the shot. The hand farthest away has been carried low in order to slap at the dribble; therefore, it is brought up from underneath in an attempt to lift the shot, or, if the float shot is employed, this hand is in excellent position to block the shot.

9. *Blocking the jump shot at the end of the dribble.* The guard is trying to maintain good defensive position during the dribble. Then, as soon as the dribbler brings both hands in contact with the ball, the guard must close with him and attempt to block the shot with the hand farthest away from his opponent. This should result in rotation of the body with the guard facing his opponent. If the opponent stops and fakes, the guard will land in a crouched position between his opponent and the goal. As one hand goes up to block the ball, the other hand is carried at the height of the diaphragm.

10. *Position of side man guarding opponent who does not have ball.* Use low crouch. The distance from the opponent is determined by: (1) the relative position of the ball and the opponent, and (2) the relative speed of the guard and the opponents. Crowd him, anticipate, and float. Face the opponent, but always see the ball whenever possible. If opponent is to your left (back to goal) then your left foot is between him and the basket, while your right foot is toward center court (a square stance facing opponent). The hands are up at shoulder height. Keep inside, force all play to the outside.

11. Don't leave your feet on bluff shots.

12. Do not be a "ball-hawk." Do not commit yourself.

13. Do not be caught flat-footed.

14. If offensive man drives in to the basket for a lay-up shot, hit the ball from underneath. Do not reach over him, since you will foul.

15. Watch for opposing guards breaking through on tip-off.

16. Never go on offense unless someone protects your move.

17. If you are not a good scorer then earn your way by preventing the star opponent from scoring.

18. Always hustle back; you are never too late on defense.
19. Always form a defense about the goal first. Be very sure there is no unguarded opponent between you and his goal.
20. Concentrate on a line between the ball and the goal. When the ball is passed behind a defensive man, he should drop back and concentrate on this line.
21. Cover the possible receivers. The closer a receiver is to the ball, the closer the defensive man must play him.
22. Float only on the side away from the ball, and then float only if forced to do so.
23. Away from the ball, play: (1) the ball, then (2) your opponent. On the ball, play: (1) your opponent, and (2) the ball.
24. Switch only when necessary. Keep the center closed and force all screens to the outside. The man being screened does not call the switch.

   A. Out in front and on the sides, on close crosses, come shoulder to shoulder and remain in this position until the ball is definitely on the outside. Neither the man with the ball nor the man without it should be permitted to go between the two defensive men. The same applies when out man hits post and uses guard cross.

   B. When we feel that we can fight these screens (And, frankly, in 90 per cent of the cases, if a boy is determined enough, he can fight them.), we use this rule: Stay tight on the man with the ball and loosen up on the man without the ball.

25. Keep between the opponent and the ball on cross-court cuts. If no pass is made to the cutter, and the cutter continues across to the other side of the court, the guard keeps ahead of him until the offensive player crosses the imaginary line that connects the ball and the goal.
26. If their pivot man goes to the corner, we play him eight or ten feet away until the ball approaches his area; then we tighten up.
27. On an attempted interception that fails, the teammate nearest or next in line must fill the vacated position. The player who attempted the interception must take the vacated spot left by his teammate.

28. Guard the player in front of you. Don't worry about the man behind you.

EXCEPTION: Play in front of your man in the goal area.

EXAMPLE: All men—guards and forwards— must learn to do this, as well as your pivot man.

Defensive rebounding

Establish defensive triangles with one man in front of the goal, one on either side, and two men on the foul line. These are their areas of responsibility.

1. As soon as opponents shoot, every defensive man attempts to block out. Men outside the twelve-foot area retreat one or two steps facing opponent on a line between opponent and basket. As opponent cuts for basket, make a front pivot in order to get your body between opponent and basket.

2. If opponent does not cut for basket, wait until ball can reach goal; then turn and play the ball or cover your area.

3. Men inside the twelve-foot area may use either a front or reverse pivot, since we expect them to be very close to their opponent in this area.

4. As possession of the ball is gained we split immediately up the middle to start our fast break. Take one, two, or three dribbles; then pass ahead to the side man. We feel that you leave behind one, two, or three opponents by starting up the middle on the dribble, rather than trying to get the immediate outlet pass.

18

Seven Cardinal Principles of Defensive Play

Some people maintain that defensive basketball is neglected nowadays, in view of the big scores. I do not believe this is true. We are working harder today on defensive play than we ever did in the past. This is primarily due to the fact that there are very few new defensive techniques, while offensive techniques have completely outrun those of thirty years ago. Any coach who has been in the business for that long a time will recall that anyone who took a one-handed shot thirty years ago would immediately have been labeled a "show-off."

From an offensive standpoint basketball players today are far superior to the players of fifteen years ago. But this does not mean that they are better—for, had the boys of fifteen years ago had the advantage of the knowledge that is being given to our boys today, they would have been equally as great.

To anyone who believes that present-day defensive basketball is not sound I would like to address the following questions:

How do you instruct your defensive men to guard against the hook shot?

How do you instruct your defensive men to guard the pivot man on the step-in-step-out hook shot?

How do you instruct a defensive man to guard the running jump shot?

How do you instruct your guard to stop the dribble-stop-jump shot?

I believe that after you have answered these questions to yourself you will come to the same conclusion that I have: namely, that our offensive techniques have simply outrun our defensive techniques.

The low scores of several years ago do not necessarily indicate that better defense was employed. Far from that. A low score at the end of a basketball game today does not necessarily mean that it was a great defensive game. It may have been a poor offensive game.

How many shots were taken?

How long did it take the team to set up a play?

Was ball control permitted?

Was an attempt made deliberately to withhold the ball from play?

The answers to these questions may be the answers to the lowness of the score. Scores have continued to go up; but I think that this is primarily due to the greater number of boys who are playing basketball today and to the far better facilities for teaching the game.

I believe that in defensive play we have *Seven Cardinal Principles* of play. Whenever your team plays a game it would be well for you to check to see whether you have neglected any of these principles. Defensive play is not appreciated by too many spectators and coaches today. It is unspectacular and therefore disregarded. Let me say this: I believe that, if you will check the teams that have been outstanding year after year, you will find that soundness of defensive play is responsible in large measure for their success. Their coaches know that, on an evening when the offense is not clicking, they can still save the game if they have good defense. But, if they haven't good defense, the ballgame is lost.

It is not difficult for us to teach our boys defense. They realize its importance. Our boys are convinced without a doubt that our defense will save us on the nights when our offense isn't working. A boy must be taught to realize the importance of defensive play, individual as well as team play. We possibly spend half as much time defensively as we spend offensively. Few teams spend anywhere near that much time teaching defensive play. That is the reason why I mention this. In 1955 I watched a high school game featuring a team that had scored over 100 points on nine different occasions. It was the second round of a tournament play-off; and the opposition was a good defensive team, but not a great one. The first team took a humiliating defeat, showing up at the end of the first half with only three field goals. Their opponents completely demoralized them defensively. Everyone was dumbfounded after the game, but this fact was evident—the superior defense of the one team had turned the tide into a rout.

Let's consider the *Seven Cardinal Principles*:

1. Cut down the number of shots

You've always heard the saying, "Make enough shots and the percentage will take care of you." That may be true; so the first thing to do is to cut down the number of shots you give the other team. In going back over our shot charts for a period of five years, we have found a very reliable trend in the number of shots taken. The first thing to do in defensive play is to prevent the opponents from taking a shot at the basket. They still must shoot to score. If, by aggressive defensive play, you can eliminate the number of scoring opportunities that the other team gets, you will eliminate the danger of a high score.

2. Cut down the percentage of shots

We tell our boys to be aggressive at all times. It's hard, tough work; but a lot of boys like to play that kind of ball. It's a rewarding thing to have one of your boys come up to you and ask to be assigned to guard the outstanding player on the opposing team. Several years ago we had such a boy. He wasn't interested in how many points he scored, but he liked to take a player on the other side who had a 20-point average and whittle him down to 7 or 8. The smile of satisfaction on his face after a game was always a complimentary reward. And usually before he left the dressing room he would come and ask, "Have I got Smith Saturday night?"—Smith being the star on the opposing team.

If you can force a team to take hurried, off-balance, inaccurate shots, you will destroy the shooting percentage that this team has been getting. And this is entirely the difference between aggressive defense and defense that permits a team to get good shots. When a coach comes up after a game and says, "We couldn't hit tonight," maybe there was a reason.

3. Cut down everything under eighteen feet

I like to put this in, since it fits well into the philosophy of collapsing or floating defenses. It certainly is in their favor. If you will draw a circle eighteen feet out on the floor from the basket and attempt to cut down everything in that area, getting all the rebounds, you'll have a foolproof defense. I realize this is impossible; but the fact still remains: don't give them a shot close in to the basket!

These defensive assignments are goals toward which you should work. And if you can imprint upon the minds of your boys that they must not give the opponents these close-in shots, they will get the idea and work toward this goal.

4. Cut down the second shots

A good defense should not permit a team to get the second and third shots at the basket. True, it is difficult at times to get the rebound. But the first thing in defensive play, after a shot has been taken, is to see that your individual opponent does not get the rebound. You should block out these players and then, after you have them out of play, go for the rebound yourself. If you permit the second shot and possibly the third shot, one of these is apt to fall. A good, tough rebounding team will not permit these additional shots after the initial attempt has been made.

5. Cut down the cheap baskets

How many times have you seen a good, well-played game— and then seen a cheap interception, with the boy going all the way and scoring? Did you ever see a jump ball on your own free-throw line, with the opponents slapping the ball over the head of your defensive player and going all the way to score? How many times have you seen a pass in under the opponents' basket inter-cepted and laid in for an easy basket? How many times have you seen a ball fall aimlessly to the floor and the opponents throw it in for an easy basket? How many times have you seen an opponent rebound and get an easy basket after a missed free-throw? These are just examples of cheap baskets that teams sometimes get with the minimum of effort. Some are due to carelessness; some are due to bad judgment; but in a well-played game with opponents of equal ability the deciding factor is sometimes a cheap basket at the critical time.

6. Point the ball on all long shots

As the ball is maneuvered on the outside of the defense, the defensive man playing the man with the ball should always be tight. Two of the *Cardinal Principles* are to cut down on the number of shots and on the number of good shots. If you will allow good long shooters to get set unmolested, they'll ruin you from out on the floor. Therefore, the man with the ball should always be "pointed." This is true even in floating defenses. In strict, tight man-to-man defensive play this should always be true.

7. Prevent the ball from going to the pivot

I believe that most teams feel exactly as we do. Never let the ball go in to the pivot man. If you do, their screen can be set without worrying about handling the ball. We permit the ball to go to the side of the floor, but always play to prevent the ball from going to the pivot man. As soon as the pivot man has the ball you have a dangerous offensive center. If the pivot man should be a big, husky fellow, he can take a hook shot, jump shot, or jump flip shot. He can fake on one side and go to the other. He can pass to a cutting teammate that has been freed by a screen. The ball is in an extremely dangerous position when it is held by the man playing what is normally called the pivot position. The greatest percentage of attempts at the basket are made from this position.

It has merely been my attempt to give you the results of our experience down through the years. On those long nights that are sure to come during the basketball season it is well to check on these *Seven Cardinal Principles* and see whether any of them might prove helpful to your team. It is merely a series of checks that you can rigidly apply; and somewhere along the way you will find your difficulty. Even if your team is going well, that is the time to check. Apply it not only to your plays; apply it also to your individual players. The offensive star of your team may not be the star of your team after all. His defensive ability may be so indifferent that it is causing your team to lose ballgames, in spite of the offensive contributions that he is making.

Bear this in mind, for I repeat it thousands of times to my boys each year: Your defense will save you on the nights when your offense isn't working.

19

Team Defense, Man to Man

In the evolution of the game of basketball, team defense has perhaps been the first phase of the game to complete the cycle. If there is such a thing as history repeating itself, it certainly is doing so in defensive basketball.

In the early days of the game guards stayed back and were strictly defensive men; they were the watchdogs of the basket. It was up to them to see that no one scored. They were usually the most rugged and the least versatile players on the floor. Sometimes they failed to go beyond the center of the floor on an offensive drive because they had little to do with the offense. They were not required to shoot as they did not have opportunities to do so in a game. When the opponents brought the ball down into scoring territory these two guards immediately took charge of the two forwards, the center took the opposing center and the defense was of a man-to-man nature. They played their opponents all over the floor. The opposing guards did not enter into the scoring threat and, therefore, the forwards had little to do in the defensive pattern but merely waited until their own guards got the ball off the backboard and passed it out to them.

After some years of this type of play, the opposing guards started to crash through on the offense and then it became necessary for the forwards to become defensive men. At this stage in the development of the game the five defensive men retreated to the area near the center of the floor. The first two offensive men who broke through were taken by the guards. The center was usually assigned to guard the center, then the forwards picked up the other two men. This meant that a defensive man did not always guard the same player. This method of play gradually flowed into the zone defense and the reason for it is apparent. The two big men, or the guards, were back, so that just left them there as watchdogs under the basket and gave them a particular area or zone to cover. The center played up around the front of the free-throw circle with the two forwards on each side. Then they were given a zone to cover also and the first development that took place was the 3-2 zone. The players were shifted to protect the zone into which the ball was passed. The idea at that time was to play the ball, and not the man.

Players were then taught to shift zones and every kind of zone defense known today was an outgrowth of these early principles. The zone defense was the dominant type of defense used from 1917 to 1928 and during this time it found its greatest era of prosperity. If a coach had a powerful offense, rangy players, and two good guards, he could afford to take a chance on this type of game.

In basketball the entire game is based on having individuals better than the opponents' or on being able to out-maneuver them by getting a favorable player balance against their defense. By that we mean getting 2 on 1 or 3 on 2. Since it is necessary to put three men through the first defensive line in order to beat a zone defense, it is easy to understand that when a ball is intercepted the team employing a zone defense has three men who can crash against the opponents' two guards. This is a big advantage in the zone defense.

Then came the next development in basketball which took the steam out of the zone defensive principle. A team would get a comfortable lead and when it did, it held the ball in the back court or out in front of the zone defense. If the team behind in the score wanted to win it was necessary for them to abandon the zone principle and go out and take their opponents man to man. If they were not properly schooled in this type of defense they were, naturally, cut to ribbons as the other team used crashing tactics and aggressiveness to advance the ball.

There have been many stories of games that were played in which a zone defensive team refused to come out, and the offensive team sat on the floor and held the ball. One of these games was played in the finals of the A.A.U. Tournament in Kansas City in 1927. The Hillyard team defeated the "Ke-Nash-A" team by a score of 29-10. The Hillyard team had possession of the ball with sixteen minutes of the last half to go. In fact, they held the ball in the back court and the opponents made no effort to get it. With ten minutes of the game still remaining, the crowd started to leave. The Hillyard team had a lead and had scored 29 points so they certainly could not be blamed for their tactics. The other team was behind; if they had wanted to win they should have made an effort to get the ball. A team should make an honest effort to win. The spectators could not be blamed for leaving since they came to see action.

It was in this era that the zone defense reached its greatest effectiveness, and just as an interesting sidelight, may I give you these figures? This same team won the 1926 National A.A.U. Tournament with an average of 39 points per game and a defensive average of just a little better than 21. In 1927 they repeated their championship with an offensive average of 34 points a game and a defensive average of only 20 points. They held their opponents to an average of eight field goals per game for the entire season, or an average of one goal every five minutes. Compare that today with the teams that we have had here at the University of Kentucky, which have averaged 80.7 points per game in the last five years against the best competition in America and which have established a 137-game won record and a 14-game loss record. Our defensive average for the five years was 59.1, which shows a considerable change in the game during the past twenty years.

Of course the elimination of the center-jump has had much to do with the change but the game has had tremendous offensive development since that time. The defense has also kept pace, because today whenever a basket is scored the opponents immediately get the ball and have an opportunity to score also. In the old days the ball was always taken back to the center to be jumped again. When these ball-holding tactics were used, a team brilliant on offense but weak in the man-to-man style of play that could not come out of its zone to handle such a situation could be defeated by a mediocre ball club. Such a situation cannot occur today if a team is well drilled in defense and has a proper balance with its offense.

After many years of this stationary defense a new rule was introduced requiring the offensive team to advance the ball over the center line ten seconds after gaining possession of it. This has been a help to the exponents of zone defense and, as a result, many teams have gone back to using it. This is especially true of teams that play on narrow courts.

Many coaches today say that "the best defense is a good offense" and that "the opponents can't score when we have the ball." How often have you heard those two statements? There is truth in both of them but it is not the whole truth. A good offense with a weak defense will not win ball games against a team with both a good offense and defense. And again, even though the opponents can't score when you have the ball, are you absolutely sure that you can score?

If there is anything that gives comfort and confidence to a coach it is the knowledge that his team is good defensively. On nights when the offense fails, your defense, if it is a good one, will save you. I feel that a good defense is one of the biggest factors in a team's success. On certain nights your offense will work, your shooting will be good, you will make such a high percentage of your shots that your defense is not needed. However, there will be other nights when, due to some reason that is hard to explain, the shots will not drop and it appears that you could not buy a basket if you had all the money in the world. At such a time your defense will prove a stabilizing factor and will enable your team to stay in the ball game. If you have a good defense and it can hold your opponents, it may even enable you to win despite the poor showing that is made by you offensively. A good defense will also enable you to reduce the offensive margin that a superior team may hold over you.

Many boys, as a rule, do not like to play defensive ball as it is unspectacular and is really hard work. However, on the nights when your defense has been a contributing factor in a victory the boys learn to appreciate its place in the game. Even to the spectators the word "teamwork" only applies offensively. You will hear them say: "Did you see our team pass tonight?" "Wasn't that shooting great?" "They had wonderful teamwork." We agree. But if spectators really want to see a team with good teamwork they have an excellent chance to see it on defense, though usually it is not appreciated there since the spectators watch the man with the ball.

The cycle has now been virtually completed. The present tendency in collegiate play is a return to man-to-man defense; some teams are now playing it all over the floor. We are of the opinion that the best defense is a strict, aggressive man-to-man defense. We manage to play the best ball in those games where we are tough defensively.

We do not make it a practice to work defensively during the first three weeks of practice. We work offensively because we want to give our boys complete confidence in our offensive setup. Several years ago I told our boys in the first organized practice session, "I feel that we have a lot of good material and I certainly hope that we get the maximum out of it. I want to set this as a goal for the year: Our offense needs no improvement, but I want to improve the individual defense twenty-five per cent and the team defense the same." We worked hard defensively the two weeks prior to our first game. Our boys were so anxious to make good that in the first five games, although we usually set our defense at the center line, the boys went out and without orders picked up the opponents all over the floor.

After about five minutes of the first game had gone by I turned to my assistant on the bench and said, "What has gotten into our boys tonight? We didn't tell them to play that way."

"They're doing all right," he replied. "Let's see if they can keep it up."

The boys played that way all night. They made some mistakes but their aggressive style enabled us to get possession of the ball many more times than if we had used a retreating defense. I cannot emphasize too much aggressive play because we are positive that any other style will not bring championship teams. On the nights when we feel that we are tough defensively it just simply means that all of our boys are on their toes, diving for loose balls, knocking down passes, tying up opponents with the ball, rebounding viciously, cutting at terrific speed, and in general, beating our opponents to the punch. Time and again this past year, not due to the fact that we had superior material but due alone to our aggressive style of play, we had scored over fifty points by half time against opponents that prior to game time were rated as our equals.

It is true that we had more depth in our positions than some teams but when the first team goes out and acquires a lead of 25-4 after seven minutes of play, that is not due to depth but to our superior ball handling. We feel that it is our defense that makes our offense click.

In line with history's repeating itself it is our style now to pick up the men and stay with them defensively, sometimes all over the floor and at other times on the half-floor without shifting. It is our genuine desire that some day it will be possible for us to have such good individual defensive men that we can immediately pick up our opponents and play them tight all over the floor. We believe it will have a demoralizing effect on the opponents as in most systems of play the organization is not accustomed to such tactics. Even if a team should get out in front and hold a lead for a goodly portion of the time, it is our belief that before the forty minutes of play are completed, our aggressiveness would wear them down and enable us to win.

In our practice sessions we spend time each week picking up our opponents all over the floor. We instruct our second team to pick up our first team. Whenever both teams do that during the course of an afternoon it makes for a rugged style of play, and it enables us to get in a lot of good, sound basketball instruction that we would not get in with a retreating defense.

"Meet them at the line and don't let them handle the ball" is one of the last instructions we give our boys before game time. It is our belief that the next big development in basketball will be along these lines and it will make for a much more spectacular game than the style employing a zone defense or a sinking defense.

There are many theories of offense and defense in basketball. We respect all theories and opinions for, as has been said before, no one has mastery of the knowledge of basketball. Everyone has the same information. The difference is in its application. Basically, here is what we believe in at the University of Kentucky as a team defense.

We like to play a strict, aggressive man-to-man defense, picking up the opponents' guards at the center line and fighting them there for the ball. We do not believe in shifting for this reason; if you tell a team that they should shift they will have a tendency to do that whether they are screened or not, always feeling that someone else will pick up their man. We loosen up defensively on the man who does not have the ball, and allow the defensive man on the cutting man or the man with the ball to have the right of way.

Our theory is: WE NEVER SHIFT except (and a very small "except") WHEN THERE IS A POSITIVE BLOCK. We do not shift more than four or five times during a game and sometimes not at all. I have heard our boys say, "You take care of your man and I'll take care of mine." That is the philosophy I want them to have. It makes them aggressive, it keeps them on their toes, and that is one of the secrets of our play.

The defense occurs on a man before he gets the ball, not after. Yet, how often have you seen a defensive man allow an offensive man to catch the ball, then slide up and try to guard him? Our men guarding the forwards on the side of the floor will line up right beside their men, not behind. We tell them, "Put the heat on; don't let them handle the ball. If you allow them to move the ball you won't have a chance to beat them."

I was very much interested in hearing the reaction of a high school coach who witnessed one of our games. He made this statement:

"I have never seen another team use a continuity or figure eight defense."

We will honestly say that we haven't either, but the thing that sold this coach on our defensive pattern was the fact that we were going with our men, loosening up on our screens, and never shifting.

It is absolutely necessary for the center also to stay tight in a situation of this kind. There is no use in four men fighting hard to throw a team off balance, to make them throw bad passes, to confuse them on their pattern of play, and then to have the fifth man on the team loafing on his job. It is vital for everyone to be aggressive in this style of play.

In the forward and guard assignments on team defense, all of the individual defensive requirements explained in Chapter 16 are essential.

Guarding the pivot man

Many styles of play are built around a big man who is usually placed near the basket where he establishes a pivot position. Despite the three-second rule * that restricts him, we still have a definite defensive problem. The big factor in guarding this pivot man is that the defensive man be alert. He should know where the ball is at all times. He should never relax. He must be careful that the pivot man does not get position on him. By this we mean that he should play the pivot man in such a way that the other opponents will have difficulty in passing to him. Many of these pivot men have a pet mechanical shot they like to execute. If the pivot man is playing outside the foul circle and to the side of the basket, the chances are that he is looking for the ball in order to execute one of his pet shots. Do not play behind this man. Play him strongly to the side and perhaps even in front of him. Keep your hands up to prevent him from catching the pass. Do not permit him to

---

* "A player shall not remain for more than 3 seconds in that part of his free throw area between the end line and the farther edge of the free throw line while the ball is in control of his team."—Rule 9, Section 11, 1.

back you up or push you under the basket in order to get a better shot.

If the pivot man moves away from the basket to the side, watch him. He may be a good shot from there, or he may be going out to establish a back screen in order to free a teammate. Remember, any man going away from the basket is not particularly dangerous and you should loosen up on him to pick up a man who may have been freed due to a screen. If you see that the pivot man is going sideways to screen, warn your teammates immediately. Remember, talking is part of all defensive play.

If your opponent stands in the circle in front of the foul line, play strongly to the side where the ball is. Try to prevent him from getting the pass. Be careful that he doesn't make a quick body fake to make you commit yourself and then reverse and take a high float pass under the basket. If he catches the ball, then drop behind him immediately. Don't crowd him too strongly from behind from one side, as it is virtually impossible for you to take the ball away from him. If you crowd him, he may use his foot opposite the side that you are on in a back swing in a wrapping movement, then by means of a dribble cut back to the basket. It may be necessary to loosen up as this prevents him from reversing and, at the same time, enables you to switch to pick up one of his men who may have been freed and who is cutting by him for a feed pass. Usually a pivot man will not shoot from out there, atlhough there are many excellent shots in the game who will shoot from that position. Your scouting report will give you this information.

If you have been forced to switch to take another man, you may find a situation where a small, five foot, ten inch man is guarding this big pivot man. Try to switch back as quickly as possible and do not allow your opponents to pull you out on the floor because, as sure as you do, the ball will be thrown in again allowing the big center to go to work on your small man who is probably not accustomed to guarding a big pivot man.

This will show that we play our center strong on the side where the ball is expected to come in to the pivot man. When the pivot man is as far out as the free-throw line, we play strongly to the side. If the pivot man should move back there is a possibility that we will play in front of him. The only player who loosens up will be

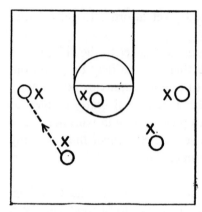

Chart 62. This illustrates how we like to carry out our defensive assignments. The position of the ball has been moved to the side of the floor in order to show how little we loosen up.

the opposite forward guarding in front, away from the ball. All others remain tight.

To the reader it may appear that this is an easy defense to block out. It would be if it were not aggressive and if our boys did not possess pride in their defensive ability. This enables us to assign our men according to size, according to speed, and according to ability.

Defense after shot

When a shot has been taken, the defense does not relax; it is the responsibility of every player to keep his man out of the rebounding play and not permit him a direct path to the basket. This is done by every man keeping an eye on his opponent and waiting to see what move he makes first. As soon as he makes his initial move, turn squarely in front of him; keep in front of him by maintaining a position between him and the basket. Then in order for him to rebound he must cut around you, and usually by throwing him off a step or two you can destroy his timing for the rebound. Do not turn your head and watch the ball. Watch your opponent and see what he plans to do. We tell our boys, "Keep your man out then go get the ball." As soon as you have determined where the ball will go, stay in a crouched position so that you have an abundance of leg spring, then jump as high as you can and catch the ball. Bring it down, alighting in a crouched position. Keep your feet under you so that the opponents charging in for the ball will not make you change your stance.

Never bat the ball in defensive territory is one of our fast rules. Take the ball away from the danger zone as quickly as possible. Look over your shoulder and if you can get it out to a teammate, get it out as quickly and as far as you can. If you don't see anyone to whom you can pass, take a quick slide dribble to the side of the floor and look for one of your teammates cutting over for the pass. The big thing to remember is this: Get the ball away from the opponents' basket as quickly as possible. That is the secret of starting a fast break.

The reason we like the man-to-man defense is that it fosters individual responsibility and a desire to outplay an assigned opponent. Almost every team has one player who is an excellent offensive man. You will always assign the best defensive man to him. On our team in 1948 this man was Kenneth Rollins. He was fast, aggressive, an excellent ball handler, and a boy with tremendous pride. He knew that I had complete confidence in his defensive ability. All of his teammates believed in him. It placed a responsibility on him and, at the same time, gave him confidence. For someone to outwit him and score against him was a serious offense as far as he was concerned. I have heard him say, "I'm not going out here before all these people and let a man make a monkey of me."

After a game we always like to pass out the credit where it is due. On a winning club, the morale is especially high. Rollins would come in after his shower and say, "Who do I guard next?" He knew he would get the toughest assignments. After several seasons of play he usually knew far in advance every man that he would guard. He studied them carefully and made this a matter of record.

We do this on many of our opponents that we play over a period of years. After a game the coaches and the players sit down while the game is still fresh in the minds of each and make notes on all of our opponents. It is a strange thing but even though you think you can remember from one week to another just how a team plays, you would be surprised how often you find something that is very important by referring to your notes. So it is a good idea for each of the boys to keep individual notes on the players they are guarding. This comes in doubly handy if a regular should be injured in a return engagement, for the substitute can have the benefit of this first-hand information.

A man-to-man defense is adaptable to any type of offense and is particularly good for a delayed or a mechanical type of play, or one that employs spread formations. I cannot emphasize this too strongly: If you allow a team to handle the ball the way they wish to, they are certain to beat you. We realize that some of these statements are a repetition, but the purpose is to under-line the fact that they are important.

Playing a good defense all over the floor often increases the tempo of the opponents' offense far beyond the ability of their players. It causes them to get excited, it forces them off balance, and makes them throw bad passes. In a style of play where the opponents have one man who is particularly weak offensively, it may permit you to loosen up on this man and "two-time" another offensive player. Playing tight all over the floor permits the teaching of individual defense with only one team-play element involved, that being a shift on screen plays; and we try to fight through those if at all possible. This, in detail, is the way the University of Kentucky's defensive pattern operates.

Shifting man-to-man defense

In this type of defense we find a combination of the strict man-to-man and the sinking type of defense. Whenever a screen is made, the defensive men always shift opponents. It is not nearly as aggressive as the man-to-man type of play and, therefore, does not attain as many pass interceptions. The theory here is that players cannot fight their way out of screens and the easiest way to handle the situation is to shift. Some coaches use this shift on every screen or on every potential screen. We taught this style of play here at the University of Kentucky for many years but, invariably, we ran into this situation at half time in the locker room.

We would have a situation where both defensive men wound up with the same opponent and allowed the other to go toward the basket unmolested. When I would ask one of the boys what happened in a specific play, he would say, "I took Jim's man because he was blocked or was about to be blocked." Jim would say, "I wasn't in any danger at all; I could have fought my way through." Now who is responsible for such a condition? You must be responsible in team defense and here was a situation where one boy came to the aid of another only to find that his help was not needed at all.

Never forget one important thing: On a positive block you must talk and shift, but whenever possible loosen up and run through. That is the theory we have been forced to adopt here at the University of Kentucky because we feel that under the shifting man-to-man defense we could not get the desired responsibility and the aggressive play that we wanted.

Sinking man-to-man defense

In this type of defense we begin to flow into the zone principle. The defensive man on the side of the floor opposite the ball will sink to help strengthen the defense around the basket.

It can be seen in Chart 63 that the principle in this defense is similar to the zone. It cuts off plays going around the pivot man (No. 5) as the opposite forward and guard have moved over there definitely to strengthen that area.

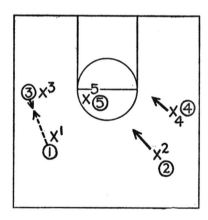

Chart 63. Here is shown the sinking man-to-man defense when the play is on the left-hand side of the floor. As the ball moves in that direction (from No. 1 to No. 3), the forward on the opposite side of the floor (X2) will retreat to a position in front and to the side of the pivot man (No. 5). The opposite guard (X4) will move to the side and behind No. 5. This chart illustrates a strong defense and, of course, is based on the fact that the team employing it feels that the opponents cannot move the ball fast and that they cannot shoot well from out on the floor.

Several years ago we were defeated in a very important game by this type of defense. It was true that the defense bothered us, but it is also true that we only hit three baskets out of forty-one attempts in the last half. That combination brought to an end a twenty-eight-game winning streak. Possibly I may add, not in the nature of an alibi, that we were not mentally up to the game. Our goal shooting certainly indicates that. Our defense was good enough and kept us in the game all the way, but our offense failed miserably. Since then the word has been passed around that to beat our team it is necessary to withhold the ball from them and to use a sinking defense. In fact, almost every team that we have played in the last two years does exactly that. Now we feel that this is a standard pattern of play that will be found in almost every game. In fact, should we meet the other, it would perhaps upset us since we have not been in the habit of meeting any other style in recent years.

Full-court press

A. Use switching man-to-man to create as many double-teaming situations as possible.

Drills

1. Pick up at endline.
2. Double-team the in-bounds man.
3. Pick up at sideline.
4. Pick up on out-of-bounds at center line.
5. Pick up after your free-throw.

B. We attempt to invite our opponents to cross with each other, thereby creating an ideal double-teaming situation.

C. We press in only *three* situations:
   1. When we are behind late in the game.
   2. When our opponents are using a deliberate attack and and we believe that by speeding up the tempo we can disorganize their attack.
   3. When we do not respect our opponents' ball-handling.

20

Zone Defense

Where the principle of man-to-man defense is to play the man, the principle of zone defense is to guard a specific area and play for the ball. The purpose of the zone defense is to prevent an offensive team from scoring by playing the five defensive men in a movable unit between the ball and the basket.

Three-two shifting zone

This was the earliest development in the zone defense. It employed three men out and two under the basket. Usually, two big men were placed behind with the center in the middle of the front line, and the two forwards on each side. The center covered the area directly in front of the basket and as soon as the ball was taken off, he, by means of the fast break, cut down in a straight line for the other basket.

153

If either of the big guards took the ball off the backboard he passed out to one of the forwards. The opposite forward came down in a straight line on his side of the floor and the three men presented a three-lane fast break. This was the most popular defense used in the Middle West. Charts 64 and 65 will show this defense and the principle involved when the ball changes possession.

Chart 64. If the ball is directly in front of X2, then X2 fights to prevent a long shot, dribble, or pass in. X1 and X3 tend to play in while X4 and X5 just keep their positions.

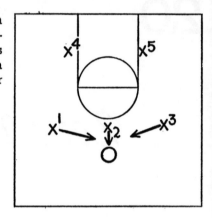

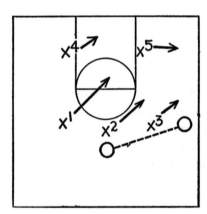

Chart 65. If the ball is passed to the side as indicated, then the defensive men shift as shown in the diagram.

Two-one-two shifting zone

In this type of zone defense the center is dropped back to a position near the free-throw line and the two forwards are brought in to tighten the gap vacated by the center when he plays in the front line. This is the most popular type of defense used today. It sacrifices some of the fast-break qualities of the 3-2 zone, but it has strengthened the rebounding possibilities. Charts 66 and 67 illustrate the 2-1-2 zone shifting requirements depending on the position of the ball.

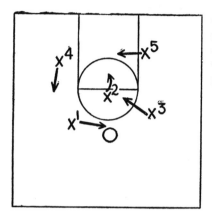

Chart 66. If the ball is directly in front, then one of the two out defensive men (X1) must cover the man with the ball. The others move in the lines indicated.

Chart 67. When the ball moves to the side of the floor, the defensive men move in the lines indicated. It will be seen that the men playing in the center will try to play in such a way as to prevent a pass from coming in to the pivot man.

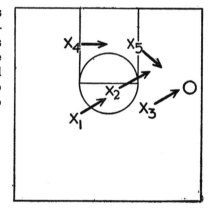

Two-three shifting zone

This moves the center directly in front of the basket and about ten feet out from the end line. The two big guards are spread and the two forwards retain relatively the same positions that they did in the 2-1-2 defense. This type of defense is especially effective when the opponents have good corner shots or when they try to get shots from the side of the floor. Charts 68 and 69 indicate the paths of the men when the ball is found as indicated in the diagrams.

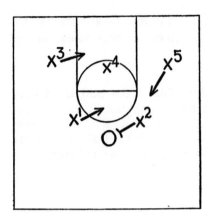

Chart 68. One of the front-line men must cover the ball. In this case, it is X2. X1 then drops back while X5 moves up to strengthen X2's vacated position.

Chart 69. When the ball is moved to the side of the floor as shown, the defensive men move as indicated. X4 is always near the basket, where he is in excellent position for rebounding.

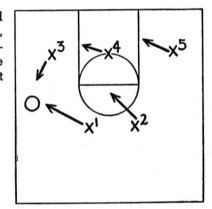

One-two-two shifting zone

This zone is also adaptable to a narrow floor. In college play this does not present a problem, but many of our high school floors are still not of standard size. It is sincerely hoped that the next development in the game will be a requirement that all floors built hereafter be of standard size.

The 1-2-2 shifting zone occurs when the one man in front is given the privilege of playing man to man.

Several years ago it was my pleasure to see a final game in a state tournament where this type of defense was used. The one man in front proved a demoralizing influence on the opponents as they had but one good man who could handle the ball. As a result of using this particular type of play, the team was able to win a championship title in a very fast class of competition. Charts 70 and 71 will illustrate the use of this zone depending on the location of the ball.

Chart 70. If the ball is directly in front, the zone will operate as indicated. X1 will fight for the ball.

Chart 71. When the ball moves to the side, X2 will fight for the ball and X1 will drop back as shown. X4 will move up to strengthen X2 while X5 will drop back in the area near the basket. X3 will drop near free-throw line.

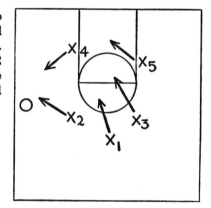

Two-two-one shifting zone

This defense is especially adaptable to a team which has a big center who can be placed directly under the basket, or to a team which has a big, awkward boy who does not shift well. It is also employed in a case where a team has a narrow floor. This defense is sometimes varied by the three men back playing zone and the two men in front playing man to man. It makes a very effective zone if the two front men are given considerable liberty as to where they play. Charts 72 and 73 will show how this zone operates depending entirely on the location of the ball.

Chart 72. If the ball is directly in front, the zone will operate as indicated. X1 will fight for the ball.

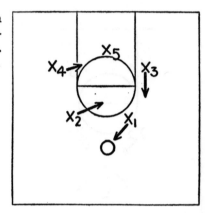

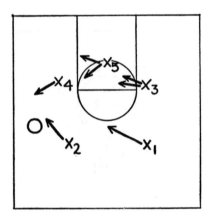

Chart 73. When the ball moves to the side, X2 will fight for the ball and X1 will drop back as shown. X4 will move up to strengthen X2 while X5 will drop back in area near basket. X3 will drop near free-throw line.

Strong points of the zone defense

1. It is effective against short shots and pass-and-cut tactics.
2. Its compactness renders it difficult for the offense to open up normal passing lanes, thus necessitating careful maneuvering and accurate passing by the offense.
3. It develops "ball-hawks" and the ability to intercept passes.
4. It conserves energy.
5. It is the best formation from which to launch a fast-breaking offensive, if that is the style of offensive play to be

stressed; and in such a case the energy saved on defense is valuable.

6. It is strong against the screening game.
7. It is strong against "free moving" offenses.
8. It tends to reduce the number of personal fouls.
9. It is especially effective on narrow floors.
10. It is compact from the standpoint of backboard recoveries.
11. It can utilize large men who are particularly well qualified for or versed in individual defensive technique.
12. It is not difficult to teach or to learn, as the shifting with the ball soon becomes automatic.

Weaknesses of the zone defense

1. It is weak against side shots and long shots.
2. It loses its mass effectiveness when spread by the offense; in such event the players using it are practically compelled to play man to man.
3. If it overshifts, it is weakened on the blind side.
4. If it fails to shift or if it is drawn out, it is weakened at the free-throw line.
5. It tends to lead to the neglect of individual defensive fundamentals.
6. It makes impossible the matching of men according to height, speed, or scoring ability.
7. It cannot, by forcing, increase the tempo of the opponents' attack.
8. It must be abandoned at the close of a losing game, when the use of man-to-man technique becomes necessary.
9. It makes possible the overloading of one zone by the opposing team, that is, the maneuvering of two offensive men into the territory of one opponent.

21

Defense Against the Fast Break

The best defensive setup to employ against a fast break is to prevent the men who wish to start a fast break from getting position. Naturally, if a team employs a zone defense it will be impossible to draw the key defensive players away from the basket and, therefore, this method is useless. The second method, and the one perhaps the most satisfactorily used, is to tie up the opponents before they can get the fast break started. A terrific rebounding game against such a team will usually pay off. Every team that employs a fast break has a definite pattern that they like to use. If you can learn this pattern by scouting a team, you can then, by vicious rebounding, tie up their men who start the initial pass and thus prevent the outlet pass from getting to the key player.

160

Defense against the fast break

Several years ago we played a team in the finals of the South-eastern Conference Tournament. They had a beautiful team with a wonderful fast break. They liked to advance the ball by bringing it out to a man at the free-throw circle; he turned immediately and advanced the ball down the center of the floor with the two other men breaking, one on each side. It is always interesting in a tournament to get the reaction of the spectators and over a four-day period a coach can get almost every viewpoint of the game. To be perfectly honest, we did not feel too comfortable about this game. However, we instructed one of our boys to play for this first outlet pass and not to allow this man to get away with the ball. We played so that we always had one of our men going to this area and at the same time we maintained three men at all times on the boards, with this fourth man assigned to cover everything directly in front of the basket. Only once during the evening were our opponents able to get away with the fast break and on that occasion they scored. We are certain that due to the fact that we tied up this outlet pass and by reason of that fact alone, were we able to stop their offensive drives. This shows the value of both scouting, and building a team so that it is able to play to the strengths or to the weaknesses of an opponent.

The other method of combating the fast break is by picking up the opponents tightly man for man immediately after the ball is lost. If the defense is instructed to play really aggressive ball, the fast break may be minimized and it will force the offense to stop and pass the ball back to the other men. Any time that you force a man in the fast break to stop and pass back, you have virtually destroyed the effectiveness of the fast break.

To meet the fast break it is well to drill your defensive men with two offensive men breaking down against one defensive man, with three offensive men breaking down on two defensive men. Where one defensive man is forced to handle two, he naturally has a situation in which his footwork and his all-around defensive ability will show up. Many times during a ball game a guard will be faced with this situation. The first thing that he must consider is the location of the goal. He must always protect the basket and must maintain a position that will prevent one of the offensive men from getting behind him. He should keep his back to his goal and should play in such a position that he is midway between his opponents. If the men crash down on him he will be forced to retreat. As their play approaches the basket he will not be able to rush out at one of the opponents because, if he does so, the other will slip under the basket, receive a pass, and score. He must, then, fight, yell, slap his feet, or use any maneuver possible to try to make one of the offensive men commit a mistake. If he can force one of them to stop, he is in a position to retreat and cover the other. If he succeeds in stopping one of the players, one of his teammates will be sure to arrive in time to help cover this man. If a teammate is rushing down to help he should take the man nearest him and allow the original defensive man to take the opponent nearest the basket. It also helps if the original defensive man talks in a situation of this kind so that the other player will understand what is expected of him.

We practice a drill for this. We place the men in lines of two under one basket. We place the defensive man on the center line. We then allow the two offensive men to advance the ball with a series of passes and dribbles at full speed, and make the defensive man cover the situation. After you have used this drill for several days then allow a second defensive man to come from the same basket where the two offensive men start at the instant when the offensive men cross the center line. In other words, try to create the situation mentioned above; that is, have one defensive man take two offensive men and try to stall them long enough for the second defensive man to arrive to help him. Be sure that the second defensive man does not leave until the two offensive men have crossed the center line and then make him dig as hard and fast as he can to get down there to help. It will surprise you how often, even from this great distance, a defensive man can get into the play and help stop a scoring threat. It will prove to the boys, conclusively: "You are never too late on defense."

This brings us to our next situation which is the 3 on 2. We like to practice this in about the same fashion creating lines of three under the basket and have the two defensive men wait for them at the center line. Be sure to insist that the defensive men stand on this center line when the play starts as you will accomplish much more by doing so than you would if you placed them back near the basket. Have the three offensive men move the ball from side to side as quickly as possible and make them run at top speed. This drill not only gives you practice in defense but also gives you practice in establishing the fast break. Thus the ball handling on it should be checked carefully. From a defensive standpoint we have found in a situation of this kind that in guarding the three men it is best for one of the defensive players to drop behind the other into an area around the neck of the free-throw lane. The man out in front will try to stop the ball. If the pass is made to the side of the floor, then the man behind drops out to cover the pass receiver, with the defensive man who played in front dropping back into the slot in the free-throw lane. Charts 74 and 75 will illustrate how we handle this situation.

Switching

By shifting or switching men we merely mean that when two offensive men cross on the floor the two defensive men guarding them will switch opponents. Charts 76 and 77 will explain how these switches should be made.

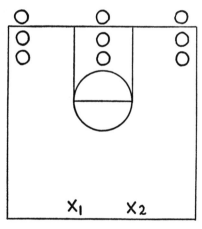

Chart 74. This chart shows the offensive men in lines of three and the position of the two defensive men. Be sure the defensive men are on the center line to begin with and then maneuver into good defensive position. The ball starts with the center offensive man. As he advances, one of the defensive men drops behind the other as is shown in Chart 75.

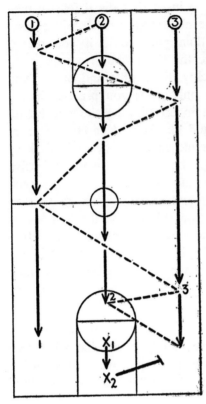

Chart 75. The ball is advanced full speed with fast passes. In this case, the defensive man X2 drops behind X1. When the ball reaches basket territory, it is passed by No. 3 to No. 2 and then quickly back to No. 3. X2 goes out to guard No. 3. X1 drops back to cover No. 2 and at the same time to prevent No. 1 from dropping under the basket for a close-in shot. This requires quick movement of the defensive men. Let the offensive men use any tactics they may choose to score. Check the fundamentals of the defensive men.

Chart 76. On the guard-around play No. 1 is using No. 2 and X2 as a screen hoping to drop off X1. In this play X2 shifts to pick up No. 1, and X1 cuts in back of No. 2 and takes exactly the same position that X2 had. Usually on this play No. 2 tries to cut around the pivot man and X1 is in excellent position to go with him.

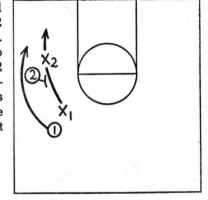

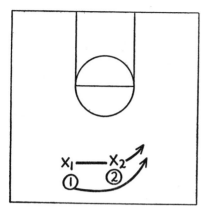

Chart 77. In this case, where No. 1 tries to use No. 2 as a screen, X1 will tell X2 to shift and take No. 1 while X1 will move over into the position vacated by X2.

Freezing or stalling

At the close of a tight game where one of the teams has but a few points' lead, it is essential to protect that lead by withholding the ball from the opponents in order to kill time. This is known as freezing the ball, or stalling. The teams that play a deliberate offense try to get a comfortable lead and then control the ball so that the minutes tick away before they surrender the ball. Naturally their plays are designed for specific situations. They make it appear that they are trying to score but all the time they are merely wasting precious minutes. If an opportunity presents itself to score, they will go in and do so. Usually an old, experienced club can handle a situation nicely this way.

However, the stall, or freeze, to which we refer is generally the one found in the last three or four minutes of the game where a team has a three or four point lead and just simply holds the ball out on the floor and moves it only enough to withhold it from the defense. A lot of fouling sometimes occurs at this stage of the game due to the fact that the defense is trying to knock the ball away from the offense. The offensive players merely take the ball out-of-bounds and try to control it again.

Every team should have a definite pattern that they employ in a situation of this kind. We use our continuity pattern, which is discussed in Chapter 16, Kentucky's Continuity Offense, to control the ball. We keep the ball out on the floor as much as possible, but all the time we are looking for another opportunity to score.

The weakness of a stalling game is that the team usually becomes entirely stall-minded and does not attempt to score. We keep our pivot man in and out of his area and, if an opportunity presents itself, we set up a regular floor play and try to run it. At these plays the defense generally gets flat-footed and there is no difficulty in running in for an additional score. In playing a fine team in the semi-final game of the N.C.A.A. Tournament, we found that we had a six-point lead with about three minutes to go. We sent instructions into the game to play slowly, cautiously, and to make our opponents come out to take us. We were able to go in on two more occasions unmolested for layup shots at the basket, and we felt that our boys handled the situation nicely.

Again we return to the point we have emphasized over and over in this book. All fundamentals are essential and if a coach has drilled his team faithfully in these, it will pay off in such critical situations. Teams that are not well drilled in fundamentals will never win outstanding championships.

Smothering, sandwiching, or two-timing

It is regrettable that no better term can be found for this maneuver but all of these terms are used in describing the play. By the movement we mean leaving one player unguarded while two defensive men go after an offensive man.

This situation may occur when the offensive team is stalling, especially when the stall has assumed routine ball handling and it is felt that the play has been diagnosed sufficiently to enable one of the defensive men to change direction and fly at an opponent who has the ball, or who is about to receive it. This term is also used to describe a play in which a team may have a star and two defensive men are assigned to watch him, leaving a weaker opponent unguarded. It also applies to the play on a pivot man where the defensive man on the pivot man plays directly behind him and, as the ball is passed in from the side of the floor, the opposite forward in the front line is dropped back to tie up the pivot man from the front.

It is a term also used to describe the play under the basket in which the ball has been taken off the backboard by a defensive man and two men move in on him from opposite directions at the same time.

We like to stay and fight for the balls on our own board. We believe that one of the best methods to combat the fast-break setup is to smother the play before it can get organized. If a defensive guard takes the ball off and to the side by means of a dribble, we like to send a man ahead to cut him off and make him reverse. We like to send a man following him so that when he pivots he will pivot directly into our man, both offensive men closing in on him. Chart 78 illustrates this movement.

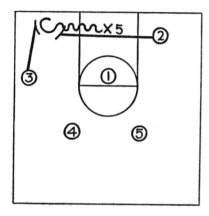

Chart 78. Here defensive player X5 takes the ball away from the backboard and, by means of the dribble, goes to the side away from the basket, hoping to pass out. Offensive player No. 3 cuts in front of him to prevent him from making the pass out and forces him to pivot. Offensive player No. 2, instead of dropping back, goes directly after him. As defensive player X5 pivots, he turns directly into No. 2 and is tied up with the ball. The move in Chart 78 is not hard to teach; and, if you will instruct your boys to stay and fight for rebounds and to smother or sandwich the man with the ball, they will not only recover a lot of balls under the basket and get held balls out of these situations, but will also discourage a defensive man from rebounding.

DEFENSE AGAINST SIDE SCREEN

Chart 79. No. 2 goes over to establish a lateral screen on X1. X2 will follow him until it is evident what No. 2 intends to do. X2 will warn X1 by telling him to "switch." X2 then will split Nos. 1 and 2 but take No. 1. X1 will fight to the inside as shown, since the ball, if it comes to No. 2, will come from that direction.

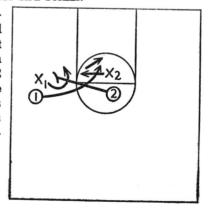

DEFENSE AGAINST DOUBLE SCREEN ON PIVOT MAN

Chart 80. This play may be handled in several ways. X3 may stay tight on No. 3 and shift only if it is evident that No. 1 or No. 2 is getting loose. X1 and X2 merely come in as indicated and switch men. Another way to handle this is to give the first man cutting the right of way. In this case X3 will loosen up and let X1 through. If a shift is made, X2 will take No. 3 and X3 will take No. 2.

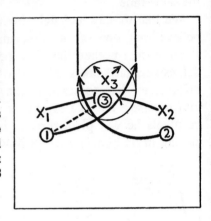

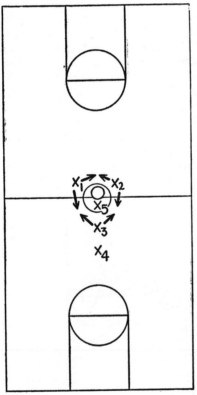

Chart 81. X5 is the center; X1 and X2 stay in close to fight for the tip-off. X3 can take either direction, whichever is indicated. Since there is plenty of time before the jump, the players can discuss the directions they will take. X4 stays back. This is known as the "Y Formation." It is also the triangle formation. In this Nos. X1, X2, and X3 revolve in clockwise or counterclockwise fashion. X1 or X2, depending of course on the direction taken, would be cutting for the ball and batting it to X4. The triangle revolves or rotates with all three men crashing.

Another case of two-timing an offensive man is when one of the defensive men has forced a dribbler to the side-lines and compelled him to execute a pivot. Another defensive man, anticipating the dribbler's next move, follows. As the man with the ball pivots, this second defensive man two-times him and ties him up.

FREE-THROW DEFENSE

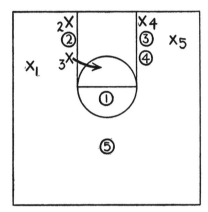

Chart 82. X4 usually is our center, since opponents will place their biggest and best tip-in man nearest the basket. X4 will try to tip back to X5. We play X5 in fairly close so he can help with the rebound. As soon as the ball hits the board or ring, X3 steps directly into the center of free-throw lane to get the ball if it falls in front of the basket and to prevent the thrower from getting ball. If it rebounds so that No. 4 gets it, then X3 can help X4 tie him up. X2 and X3 will try to tip out to X1.

HELD-BALL DEFENSE

Chart 83. The O's are opponents. The ball is on their free-throw line. We try to keep our defense between the opponents and their basket. They will line up their two guards to prevent us from getting a fast break. We do not try for plays unless we are certain of the tip. Then we try for a fast break. Otherwise we try for ball possession.

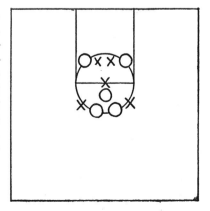

22

Substituting and Time Out

It is by means of substituting that a coach can control the game. As a general rule, we would say that if a game is going well, do not substitute and break up a winning combination. When a group of boys are turning in a good job, it is unfair to them for a coach to experiment. Substitutions should be made to strengthen the combination that is already on the floor.

When to make substitutions

However, there are situations where a coach can show his

worth by making immediate substitutions. As a coach, do not feel sensitive about what others may think of your method of substituting as it is a certainty that you understand your material better than a spectator in the crowd who may want to see one of his own pets perform. You are with the boys every day and you understand them; you know which combinations work the best. Don't let a group of spectators run your ball club for you.

A player may accumulate four fouls in the first half; we always remove him when that happens regardless of what the score may be. We do not want to go into the dressing room at the half with one of our starting players already having fouled out of the game. We feel that it hurts morale. Even though such a star player may be seated on the bench, he still has the possibility of playing in the second half. Once fouled out of the game his services have ended for that encounter. Very often after a bad first half it is possible to return this individual to the line-up in the second half and have him play the remainder of the game without committing the fifth foul.

It may be necessary for you to remove a player because he is not hitting. There are nights, and we cannot explain these, when a brilliant shooting star will be unable to connect for a field goal. Every time he shoots he will merely be inviting the opponents to take the ball. This is the place for a substitute. It may be that one of your players is taking careless or hope shots at the basket. A reward for fighting for a ball and getting possession of it should be at least a fair and decent shot at the basket. It may be that one of your players is loafing coming back on defense; the best way to cure a situation of this kind is to put a substitute in the game who will not do so. It may be that one of your men has been assigned to a much faster opponent and it will be necessary to remove him from the game and use one of your faster subs.

Again, there is the problem of fatigue. If a boy is tired a coach should be able to detect this and remove the individual. Then there is always the case of a team or an individual not being mentally up to the game. Possibly your players expected too easy a game. Removing them and letting the subs play may get them in the proper frame of mind to return to the game and play better. Remember, there is no such thing as an easy game.

The only easy games are the ones that have been played and won and are in the record books.

Calling time out

This past year we have made it standard practice to attempt to get through the first half by calling no more than one time out. No fast rule can be laid down for this but we try to call time out only if we are in trouble. We do not permit the calling of time out in order for a boy to rest. The place to rest is on the bench, not out on the floor. When our boys get tired we have them signal to us and we immediately send in a substitute. When our boys point to themselves they are merely instructing us that they are fatigued and want a few moments' rest. This allows us to keep our time-out periods for emergencies.

When should time out be called? If the opponents have a good rally under way it is always necessary to call time out. This pause not only gets your own team better organized but also has a tendency to cool off the opponents.

What does a team do during a time out? Very often you will see a team call time out, a manager run out with the towel, and about all that happens is that the players use the towel to wipe off the perspiration. Little conversation takes place. We try to utilize this time whether we or the opponents call time out, to organize our offense and defense. There may be a possibility that the men were wrongly assigned before game time. It may be necessary to switch defensive men due to either the factor of speed or the position the opponent assumes on the floor during the course of play. In other words, an opponent may have been assigned to your center and you wish your center to guard the pivot man. It may happen that when the game begins your center has been drawn out into the front line of defense and the man that you expected to play on the pivot line will not be there. It may be necessary to make a switch here immediately, and it may even be done without calling time out; the boys may decide to change assignments and that is desirable. They may ask these questions: How is one of their players getting loose? Should we shift on this screen or can we run through? Why aren't we getting the rebounds? How are they getting away on their fast break? How are we getting blocked out? These are all intelligent things to discuss during a time-out period and it is more important to talk them over than merely to take a drink of water, wipe off the sweat, and sit on the floor for a rest.

Whenever you have a good rally underway, do not call time out; make the opponent do this. Recently I watched a team stage a brilliant rally; in fact, it appeared that the team had simply caught on fire. The team play was completely organized and every single individual was playing to the best of his ability. Naturally, since the team was playing with tremendous speed and enthusiasm, one of the boys got a little tired. Instead of telling the coach to remove him so that he could put in another player and keep the game going, the boy called time out. And it was during this time out period, not only that the other team had an opportunity to become organized, but also that this player's own team cooled off. The rally ended because a player on the team that was staging it called time out. The lesson here is merely this: When you have a rally underway, keep it going.

23

Organization on Trips

It is very important that all phases of the game be well organized, practice begin at a certain time, the boys have clean equipment, and that a player fully understand what is expected of him both when he is at home and when on trips.

I think it may be well to give a report on one of my first experiences in coaching a college team. It had been my good fortune to play on a splendid college team, and so discipline was no problem. I had also coached several years of high school ball, which was a great help in coaching college ball. (To a youngster who wishes to go into the coaching profession, may we add this idea? It does not make a great deal of difference where you start; it is where you finish that counts.)

When I took over the responsibility of coaching the team here at the university, I was initiated into some of the established traditions on the very first trip. It was the custom for the novices on the squad to carry all of the equipment for the veterans. It was a new idea to me because I believed that everyone should look out for his own equipment. It was not unusual on this trip to see a sophomore carrying three bags of equipment and a veteran walking along with an overcoat over his arm. The writer was shocked when the team reported at the depot. Some of the boys wore sweat shirts and two of them showed up in knickers (then in vogue) that were allowed to hang down to the ankles. No one had a hat.

It was the custom in those days for athletes to give the impression that they were a tough lot and commanded respect merely because they were athletes. However, times have changed. Fortunately, we have a fine basketball tradition here at the university. Our big problem is to keep it going. From one end of the state to the other there is tremendous interest in everything that we do here at the university. It is difficult for us to live up to the high hopes that all these people have for us.

After the boys have enrolled in school we call a meeting on the evening of the third day, and we try to acquaint all members of our teams with our traditions and tell them exactly what is expected of them. At every university more is expected of an athlete than of a regular student. The eyes not only of the student body but also of the townspeople are on the athlete. It is merely the price that an athlete must pay for the glory that he receives.

The first thing we tell our boys is this: "If we did not feel that you would benefit by coming to the university, and if we did not feel that you could contribute something to us, we would not have you here. The main objective of your being here is to get an education. The next four years will be the most important of your life, and we want you to be sure to walk across the platform at the end of that time with a degree, and preferably a degree in an established profession. If you are studying medicine (Nine basketball players in the past twenty-one years have received medical degrees.), if you are studying engineering, or if you are studying law, naturally it will take you longer. But we prefer that you study for a specific occupation rather than merely go to college."

Today the University of Kentucky basketball team travels to the game site by means of a chartered plane. We do this for obvious reasons. We can stay in the schoolroom longer and we can usually return immediately after the game. We can play at many of our conference schools and be in Lexington from one and a half to two and a half hours after the game is finished. Since many of the schools that we play are in the Eastern Time Zone, this allows us to get back to Lexington often before 11:00 o'clock. We have a chartered bus at the Field House; and immediately after we finish dressing we take the bus to the airport. There the plane is ready and we eat a box lunch on the way home. The boys like this, and often they are in bed in Lexington before they would have been if we had stayed in the town where we played. If we play on Saturday night, we often leave Lexington after our evening meal and fly to our destination.

The rooming list has been prepared in advance and we try to assign boys the way they room here at the University. However, boys occasionally change this since they wish to study together on the trip. Bed check is at 10:30 and we get up the next morning at the regular time. Our meals have all been set up in advance.

We like to eat at twelve with perhaps a chalk talk from 1:30 to 2:00. At two o'clock we go to bed until five. We eat at 5:15 and at this meal we tell our boys to go for a short walk, report to their rooms at 6:15 and be down ready to go to the gymnasium at 6:45 (if the game is to be played at 8:00). If we dress at the hotel, we leave at 7:15.

That routine is so well established in the boys that they expect it at every game. If we make a long trip we very often have the entire schedule for each day mimeographed and give every boy a copy of it. In that way he knows exactly the names of the hotels where we stay, the trains and the time that we will leave and return. This is especially useful since some of the boys like to leave a copy of our schedule with their families. There is some comfort derived by individuals in knowing at all times where they can be reached in case of emergency. Of course our office has this information but it may not be open at the particular time the information is needed.

It has become the custom with most teams to go out to the

Field House and shoot baskets the morning of the game. Our boys like to do this because it accustoms them to playing conditions. And, after all, the home floor advantage is tremendous. I know that some people feel that coaches make too much of this; but I still believe that a boy knows his way around on his own floor a lot better than he does around a strange floor. The same is true in your own home. I can find my way to every light switch in my house on the darkest night, and can find my way from one room to another, though I doubt whether a perfect stranger could do so. But after a little practice he too might find it a little more convenient. Another reason for this morning practice is that we don't want our boys just to walk aimlessly or stand around on the streets, since we feel this takes a lot out of them. This is especially true if you play in a large city, for the boys will try to cover the entire town in a few hours.

On trips when we are away more than one day, the time factor is important. The boys have idle time on their hands. Many of them use this in studying. However, we try to help them and usually take them in a group to a show or to other wholesome forms of entertainment that may be available.

We have a fine bunch of boys and we try to provide the best for them. Our boys learn a lot in their travels. It is a part of their educational process

24

Tournament Play

Every year as the mad month of March approaches, every coach in the United States wonders about the same thing: How can I win the tournament?

Perhaps the best answer to this could be supplied by the team's record up to the time of the tournament. However, this is not always a true criterion. A good team that should win the championship is upset in the first round by a team that has had a very spotty record.

In 1934 we took to the Southeastern Conference Tournament in Atlanta a team that had been undefeated during the entire season. Only eight teams were invited. The Mississippi team had had a bad siege of the flu and was unable to participate. A last-minute appeal was made to Florida, who had a poor record for the season, asking them to fill in for Mississippi. They got their boys together and were happy to come. In the first round they knocked off Kentucky and progressed to the finals of the tournament, losing only in the last few minutes of play.

Therefore, what factors govern tournament competition? I would say that a team must not only be physically fit, but must also be mentally right for tournament play. The longer I stay in this coaching profession, the more convinced I become that a good athlete is good only if he is *mentally* right.

This is how we like to handle our tournament squad. In the ten days prior to the tournament, we wish them to maintain an absolutely strict routine. We try to arrive at the tournament with all of the boys in good mental and physical condition. We work very little five days before the tournament except on shooting and on fundamentals. In other words, we want them to be in the mental condition of *wanting* to play when they get to the tournament.

We plan to reach the tournament site about eight hours before our first game. Usually there are a lot of fans following every team. They wish the team well, but at the same time bother the kids to death. We like to keep our boys away from the crowds. We allow them to see some of the games, especially if there is a team playing that we have not played or that we have not seen play during the year. On the afternoon of the day we play, we prefer that the boys go to a show or rest in their hotel, rather than run around the streets or sit in the gym watching other teams play. When a boy is competing in athletics, it takes something out of him to sit there and watch game after game, because he is mentally playing the game too.

Should we be fortunate enough to win, we then maintain our daily routine. We get the boys up at 8:00 A.M. and feed them a light breakfast. In fact, all of our meals are lighter on the day of a game than they are at other times. What do we feed them for breakfast? We like a half a grapefruit, two scrambled eggs, two pieces of toast, and coffee or milk. We eat at 12:00 and, again, we like a half of grapefruit, a small steak, a small baked potato, peas, toast, a dipper of ice cream, and a drink.

Then we like the boys to go to their rooms at 2:00 o'clock

and take a nap. We call them at 4:30; and at 5:00 o'clock we eat a small five-ounce steak, two pieces of dry toast, and tea. We let them walk around until 6:00 o'clock and then get them off the street and back up to their rooms.

We like to dress at the hotel. If the game is played at eight o'clock, we leave the hotel at 7:15 and go immediately to the dressing room. After the game is over, we get something light to eat, and go right to bed.

All visitors are kept out of the rooms during the entire period of the tournament, and we never permit more than the two boys assigned to a room to be there at any time. All telephones are blocked and no calls go in or out of their rooms. To sum it up, we want to maintain the daily routine. We don't want the boys mentally disturbed by a lot of well-wishers, card sharks, and general nuisances.

Most teams eat too much on a trip. We like to bend over the other way; a hungry cat still catches the most mice. Then, we like the boys to get plenty of sleep and rest because it is good mental and physical conditioning and promotes a general desire to win which helps to bring success at these tournaments.

25

The Practice Week

Each week presents a different problem for a coach. The spacing of the games, the condition of his team, the location where the game will be played, examinations, and dozens of other factors determine the practice.

Let us assume that we are playing games on Monday and on Saturday. The Monday game will be played at home. If the season is well advanced, we will allow our boys to take Tuesday off. We tell them not to come near the gym, unless they have injuries that need to be treated, and to break up the daily routine as much as possible. After a game we all meet in the dressing room and I say to the boys, "We won't work tomorrow. It's a good day to catch up on your studying and courting. Report

Wednesday at 3:30." However if it is early in the season it may not be advisable to cancel the Tuesday practice session.

We observe a weekly schedule such as the one that follows:

Tuesday

3:30 to 4:00 Practice "spot" shooting.
4:00 to 4:10 Shooting over screener.
4:10 to 4:30 Fundamental guard offense.
4:30 to 5:00 Working offensive plays against tight defense; half floor.
5:00 to 5:15 Free throws.

Wednesday

3:30 to 4:00 "Spot" shooting.
4:00 to 4:15 Guards—rebounding, taking balls off basket, tying up center with defensive man, working shooting drills. Forward—faking, reversing, and rebounding.
4:15 to 4:30 Individual defensive drills.
4:30 to 5:00 Team defense.
5:00 to 5:15 Free-throwing.

Thursday

3:30 to 4:00 "Spot" shooting.
4:00 to 4:10 Shooting over screener.
4:10 to 4:20 Guard offense.
4:20 to 4:30 Running "dummy" offense for timing.
4:30 to 5:15 Scrimmage.
5:15 to 5:30 Free throwing.

Friday

3:30 to 4:00 "Spot" shooting.
4:00 to 4:20 Offensive drills against tight defense.
4:20 *for as long as necessary*. Defensive review against plays of opponents. Free throwing for 15 minutes.

We do not take time from our regular practice period to discuss our scouting notes. It will be noted that we start practice at 3:30. Since the preceding class ends ten minutes before three, we have 40 minutes before practice to go over scouting notes. If we are preparing for a particularly difficult game that presents special problems, we may have a one-hour practice on Tuesday to go ovei these problems. The chalk talks always come on Wednesday and Friday from 3:00 to 3:30. If we need to work on special situations, we keep the boys after practice. And remember, we always have a last minute chalk talk on the day of a game.

Practice will vary. I have merely presented a week of actual practice that we had early in February. This would not be a typical practice week in October, November, or December, for those very early sessions would have more and shorter fundamental drills. The shooting drill is always the same, for it should never be minimized.

26

Diet and Training Table

Until a few years ago, we did not have a training table for our basketball team here at the university. Our boys did not live together, and to some extent that is true today. Some of our players are married and live wherever they can find accommodations. Also these married students naturally eat at home and it is virtually impossible to supervise them. During the 1954–55 and 1955–56 seasons the single basketball players lived in rooms on every floor throughout the men's dormitory. We wanted them to be classified as just ordinary students and did not want them to be segregated so that they would be considered as a basketball clique. This worked to complete satisfaction, and the custodian of the dormitory told me hundreds of times that he looked upon the basketball players as the natural leaders in the residence halls. However, in the fall of 1956 the boys were given a wing in the new Residence Hall so that on days of games they would not be disturbed by other students passing by their doors, but would be permitted to get those two hours of rest in the afternoon of a game that we like them to have.

It is still difficult for us to set up a training table because our boys are in attendance at various colleges and must go to classes at all hours of the day. However, we try to have a training table at noon and in the evening. We try to eat at 12:00 noon, but sometimes it is necessary for a boy to eat at 11:00 o'clock or 1:00 o'clock, and in that case we merely keep his portion of the food available for him at those times. The evening meal can be arranged, since there are no classes to conflict with this. The training table begins the first week in December and ends the first week in March. Before and after that time, the boys are permitted to go through the line at the cafeteria and eat whatever they prefer. It is impossible to supervise the meals of the boys who eat at home, although it is our conviction that no athlete was ever hurt by eating the food prepared in his home.

In high school the diet is a still bigger factor because there the boys come from every branch of society. It must be assumed that a mother's cooking is the best.

We give our boys a wide range in the selection of their food, although after being on the squad for a short time they naturally know what foods are best for them.

Meats and poultry

We like all meat to be cooked well. We approve of roast beef, steak, lamb chops, roast veal, roast lamb, fresh fish, chicken and turkey. I wish to be perfectly honest with the reader of this book. Several foods that we list may seem improper and may shock the strict adherent to a proper diet. Although there are certain foods that we do not give them, we like to vary our meals to make them interesting. For example, on the days that we do not play and are traveling with our team, we let the boys eat fried chicken. It seems to bolster the spirit of our entire team.

Vegetables

Almost all vegetables are good. We eat celery, lettuce, white potatoes boiled or mashed or baked, asparagus, lima beans, dried beans, green beans, peas, tomatoes, and greens.

Fruits

Grapefruit, oranges, baked apples, prunes, figs, raisins, dates are all good. This last year we were grapefruit-minded. We had a half of a grapefruit for breakfast and again at noon every day that we were engaged in tournament play; it did not appear monotonous to the boys and they all enjoyed it.

Breads

We like to eat toast on the day of a game but hard rolls, wheat, rye, or graham bread are satisfactory on days that we do not play.

Beverages

We drink milk, coffee, tea, and cocoa. Again, this may shock the reader, but some of our boys drink coffee at every meal. We do not believe that coffee is as harmful as some people like to think because if it were, it is our firm conviction that the federal government would not permit its unrestricted sale in every hotel, restaurant, and grocery store throughout the length and breadth of this nation. To the writer, eating breakfast without coffee would be like an Englishman having tea without tea.

Menu — game day (game 8:00 p.m.)

Breakfast—8:30 A.M.
   1 large orange juice
   2 eggs, soft scrambled
   3 bacon strips
   2 slices of dry toast (white bread)

1 pat of butter
1 soufflé cup of jelly
Coffee or milk

Lunch—12:00 Noon
Half grapefruit, chilled
8-ounce steak, medium to well done
Large, mealy baked potato
Small serving of green peas
2 glasses of milk
2 slices of dry toast
2 pats of butter
One dip of vanilla ice cream

Pre-game meal—5:00 P.M.
5-ounce steak, medium to well done
1 slice of dry toast
1 pat of butter
Small soufflé cup of honey
Hot tea or coffee

After-game meal—10:30 P.M.
Tomato juice
Half fried chicken
Mashed potatoes
Hot rolls and butter
Garden salad
Coffee or milk
Pie à la mode

Our game-day menu varies little during the season. However, we do vary our after-game meal in order to keep the boys from becoming tired of certain foods.

Our pre-game meal is just enough food to keep the boys from being hungry. It has been said that a hungry tiger fights the fiercest. I am sure this is true; and I believe the same principle applies to boys. If they are hungry they will get out and hustle. If they are logy from heavy food, they are going to drag and loaf. The most important factor in a specific diet is regularity. The body becomes accustomed to certain foods and their intake at specific times. Any interruption of this time schedule and dietary routine will often upset the digestive system.

Miscellaneous

Soft boiled, scrambled, or poached eggs are the best. For some reason or another all of our boys prefer their eggs scrambled. Oatmeal and cereal breakfast foods of all kinds are good. Boiled rice, rice pudding, and tapioca are also on our approved list.

The thing that we tell our boys is to avoid fried and fatty foods and, above all, not to eat too much. In the early days it was the custom and the belief that an athlete had to be a rough and tough specimen and had to eat like a woodchopper. These ideas have been dispelled.

27

Duties of a Manager

A coach is fortunate if he has a good student manager. The duties of a student manager have changed a lot with the years. The early managers made the schedule for the teams, but today that function is handled by the coach or the athletic director.

The duties and responsibilities of our managers are numerous. Our managers begin as freshmen in the equipment room. They work under the supervision of the equipment man and the coach. Their first duties will be to see that all balls have sufficient air pressure, that they are taken out on the floor before practice, and returned to the equipment room afterward. We practice behind closed doors. One of the managers is responsible for seeing that all the doors to our playing floor are locked. Ten colored shirts are always brought out on the floor for every practice and these should also be returned to the equipment room after practice. We also have our manager bring some sweat clothes out on the floor so that when a player is removed from a drill or scrimmage, he can keep warm.

The junior and senior managers usually referee our scrimmages. We sometimes use freshmen and sophomore managers if they are capable. The point here is that we want all of our scrimmages refereed strictly so that our boys understand the rules. It also makes for a much better scrimmage. We have been fortunate in the selection of managers, as many of them are sufficiently qualified that they also work high school games in the vicinity during their junior and senior years on our team.

When we go on a trip it is up to the managers to help the equipment man pack the uniforms. We have a good individual leather traveling bag for each player. We do not feel that a high class team should travel around with a bunch of canvas bags of all sizes and descriptions. Plenty of sweat socks are put in this bag to allow for all practices and games on our trip. We always use the same pair of shoes in our games that we use in practice and it is up to the manager to see that each player brings his shoes and puts them in his bag before the bag is given to the player. The manager always takes one extra uniform with him on the trip to replace lost or torn equipment. If we take 12 men on a trip the manager takes 6 balls along with him.

He then checks with the trainer to be sure that the trainer has packed all of the things that they will need jointly. One of these items is paper cups. We don't want all of our boys to drink out of the same bottle or cup; that is the quickest way I know of to pass around a series of colds. We have individual paper cups on a tray and as soon as a player has taken a drink from a cup, it is removed and replaced with a clean one. As an added sanitary precaution we also take a box of Kleenex. This goes to the dressing room, it goes out on the floor with us, and frequently a player comes to the side of the floor during a time-out period and uses it.

After the game the manager helps to collect all of our property and put it where it belongs. He is the last to leave the dressing room. Each boy is responsible for his own equipment;

however, if a piece of this is overlooked, the manager picks it up. The manager and the trainer jointly check the rooms, although this is not essential since the boys know that they are supposed to be in at a certain time. By too close supervision you may give the boys the impression that you do not trust them.

The trainer and manager wake the boys in the morning and in the afternoon before game time.

Errands that pertain to the game, to the players, or to that particular trip are usually handled by the manager.

28

A Coach's Relationship to His Team

In order to have a good team, certain relationships must exist. These relationships are player-to-player, coach-to-player, and player-to-coach. Let's look at all of them. We'll start with the player-to-player relationship.

I think that many teams are broken up because of jealousies that exist among the players. This may be due to various causes. Some boys are jealous if their teammates get the best of the newspaper publicity. Some coaches blame the failure of their teams on the sports writers. I think this highly unfair. A sports writer is after the news. If one boy shows up more brilliantly than the others it's natural that he should get the best of the publicity. The winner of the horse race usually makes the story while the others follow as they finish. If a boy achieves he ought to get the credit, and a coach should see to it that this does not cause ill feeling on his team. The boys must feel kindly toward each other at all times. Have them study together and try to get them to associate with members of their group as much as possible.

I think that the ideal relationship is one in which the boys have all selfishness removed from their team play and have learned that the success of one is the success of all, where one player will pass up a shot and make a pass to another and watch him reap the glory. Basketball, like all other forms of education, should not only present a mass of knowledge but should impart a spiritual view of life so that the individual may see that there is some sense in his existence. An individual who has not learned to cooperate with his fellow players has certainly missed the greatest fundamental of the game.

The second relationship is that of coach-to-player. I believe that a coach of an athletic team has one of the finest chances for leadership that exists, and that he must realize that he is building citizens rather than ball players. The first thing that we tell our boys when they report for practice is that the greatest aim of life is to achieve and succeed. We want our boys to see that the greatest opportunity is offered to those who are prepared. We want them to study. We want them to make splendid grades. We don't care for the boy who just wants to "get by"; he will play basketball the same way. We want a boy to realize that he must fight his way to the top, that there is no such thing as a short cut. Veneer isn't worth anything. As a coach you must give proper credit where credit is due and not be partial. Treat all alike.

The third relationship is that of player-to-coach. A coach may feel kindly toward his players but the players may feel very differently toward the coach. Don't let your temper get the best of you. Don't strike a player or curse him. Don't call a boy "yellow" or a "quitter." He may be fighting his very soul out for you at the time and be giving you all that he can. Do not discuss one boy with another or brag about or degrade him publicly. All these things hurt the pride of the boys and may cause a very poor player-to-coach relationship.

Many people wonder how a team is handled before a game. Frequently I am asked that question. Since coaches differ in the methods they employ in this matter, my opinions are personal. On the day before a game we shoot baskets for thirty minutes, we run through all of our plays; we practice speed passing for ten minutes and then go over our plans for the coming game. We have been practicing accordingly for days past and we want to check to be sure that all of the players understand the plans. We may then taper off with a five-minute scrimmage and go to the showers.

On the day of the game we try to get as much rest as possible. In the games played at home we try to arrive at the gymnasium at seven, and get the necessary taping out of the way. I try to meet every boy as he comes in and ask him how he feels. The answer is always the same: "Coach, I never felt better in my life." I seldom go into the dressing room until 7:25 when all of the boys have finished dressing.

Too often a coach's locker-room address before a game is used to try to stimulate in the boys a fighting spirit. The coach talks about the importance of that particular game. His pleas are tear provoking. I often hear it said: "That coach can certainly send a team on the floor with tears in their eyes." I may be wrong but I don't care for tears in their eyes; I'd rather have baskets. I feel that there are more important things for a coach to talk about. You are matching wits with capable opponents, so let's consider how to defeat them. Go over the plan of offense. Go over the plan of defense. How will you play if they employ the zone defense? What is the starting line-up? Those are sensible things to talk about before a game.

At 7:30 we go on the floor to warm up. At 7:55 I take my starting line-up to the dressing room again. Many people believe that the purpose of this is to key up the men. Far from it. I don't want my men to go on the floor excited and nervous. I want them to have positive self-control, for in basketball you need keen judgment and cool nerves. The purpose of this return to the dressing room is to adjust equipment, possibly to wash out the mouth with water and take off the warm-up equipment. I then give the players the numbers of the men they are to guard, tell them the numbers of the plays that I think will work, and what I have observed during the warm-up period.

I seldom watch my own players warm up but try to observe the opponents. How do they handle the ball? How fast are the men? Do they have one-handed shooters, left-handed, etc.? I try to give this information on the opponents to my boys, for it's valuable. I ask if they have questions, and if they have, try to answer them. We then take the floor. I seat myself with the most likely substitutes near me. I feel that a coach's usefulness again comes into evidence at this time, for often the results of the game depend on his judgment. He must make timely substitutions, give the substitutes proper information, make necessary switches in defense and offense. True, the boys must play the game and make the baskets, but the generalship of the game lies with the coach.

The game may not progress as you expect it to. The players will make mistakes. You as the coach should not get excited. Point out these mistakes to the men on the bench. As I have often said: "If a player makes a mistake it is his fault; if he makes the same mistake again, it's the fault of the coach." After the game begins its progress lies in the hands of the coach. He should be well acquainted with the abilities of his men so that he can make proper substitutions, because the power of substitution is the most important function of the coach after the game has started. If the game fails to progress as it was planned, if the defense is not properly assigned, if the offense fails to click, then the coach must make changes. It is usually a good idea to play a conservative game to begin with for most mistakes are made when the players are overanxious and nervous. We always try to get the first tip-off and score if possible. Immediately it puts the other team on the defensive, at least mentally.

Now let's take a look in the dressing room between halves. What happens there? Some coaches waste the precious fifteen minutes delivering a high-grade oration. They attempt to inspire the team regardless of the score, telling them about the school spirit and attempting to give them the fight formula. Sometimes this is necessary. But how about the game? As soon as the first half is over, get the boys in the dressing room. Have them put on their sweat clothes to keep warm. Give them a drink of water and have some towels so that they may wash their faces. Don't jump all over them, for they are fatigued and will not pay attention. With three minutes of the fifteen-minute period gone, we begin to plan for the second half. We check the fouls and the score and give each man a report on his work. First, I criticize each man's work and then I ask the players for information regarding the men against whom they are playing. This is valuable and often allows us to run particular plays the second half that will allow us to score. We always try to save some of our plays for the second half for we know that the other coach will analyze our style of play during the rest period and plan a defense accordingly.

We next analyze the opponents' style of game. If a certain player on their team is too fast for our defensive man or if he plays in a position that does not allow us to get the best of our system, we make the necessary switch during the rest period between halves. We tell our players of the plays that we have observed, of the screens that the opponents are using, the strong points or weak points of their passing attack, their defensive weaknesses, their out-of-bounds plays, their rebound work; and in general try to plan an attack that will break down their defense, and at the same time plan a defense to stop the strong points of their offense. This usually takes up the full ten minutes and then the second half begins. If you are defeated, profit from your mistakes. If you are victorious, study the game to see why you were successful.

29

Scouting

By scouting we mean getting information about the opponents. This can be done in two different ways. You can either get your information from those who have it or you can personally scout a team or send someone to do it.

If you wish to employ the first method, you can obtain information from one of the scouting bureaus that make it a practice to compile data about all of the major teams. This practice may be necessary if the finances of a team are limited, or the coach does not have an adequate staff. However, this is not as satisfactory as on-the-spot scouting by either the coach or an assistant.

It is evident that a coach can much better plan his attack when he has definite knowledge of his opponents. It is important to know the basic things that a team wishes to do and set the defense accordingly. However, each coach has pet ideas about the things he wishes a scout to observe in an opponent, and a head coach is fortunate indeed if he can develop in his assistant the ability to get the information exactly as he wishes.

We have a regular scouting form that we give to the scouts who gather information for us. We like our scouts to watch the game very carefully in the first few minutes of play without taking extensive notes. The reason for this is that a team will definitely run in a set pattern in the early stages of a game and if a scout is taking a lot of notes he may miss many of the plays.

Here is what we look for in a team:

1. Type of offense.
   A. Fast break.
   B. Deliberate plays.
2. Do they set their plays or move into them?
3. Do they use screen plays?
4. What setup do they use for tip-off?
   A. DIAGRAM: first half.
   B. DIAGRAM: second half.
5. What setup do they use on free-throws?
   A. DIAGRAM: offense.
   B. DIAGRAM: defense.
6. How do they rebound:
   A. Offensively?
   B. Defensively?
7. Do they get set on shots?
8. Are they smart or mechanical?
9. Do they employ sleepers?
10. Held ball setup.
    A. Diagram for same.
11. Team offense.
    A. Diagram for plays.
    B. Diagram for out-of-bounds plays.
12. Team defense.

INDIVIDUAL REPORT

Name   No.   Right or Left   Ht.   Wt.   Speed   Spirit

A. Rebounding ability.
B. Position in fast break.
C. Type shot used.
D. Shooting ability:
   1. Outside.
   2. Inside.
E. Where does he shoot from?
F. Type of fakes employed.
G. Will he drive?
H. Does he prefer to go right or left?
I. Footwork:
   1. Before driving.
   2. Before shooting.
   3. On defense.
   4. Before passing.
J. Defensive ability:
   1. Weaknesses.
   2. Strengths.
K. Temperament.

We instruct our scouts to make their reports immediately after the game, as it is impossible to retain a lot of this information for a long period of time.

In the offensive pattern we want to be sure to have the plays that a team likes to work and then to find out how the individuals fit into this system. From a defensive standpoint we want to know whether there is a strong team defense or whether they depend on the individual defensive ability of the players.

We want everything on a man that we can get from an individual standpoint. We tell our scouts to be sure that they get the individual characteristics of the opponents and find out exactly what they like to do, so that a definite defense can be planned against every man. Many boys have pet moves, tricks, shots, and passes that they like to employ and we want to have this information to give our boys. If a man is particularly weak defensively we want to know that too. We want to know the temperaments of the various players and their reaction to pressure

In case you find it necessary to scout a team more than once or if you have different men to scout it, we have always found it advisable never to allow the second scout to see the notes taken by the first scout. If he studies the scouting report that is before him, there will be a tendency for him to watch for those things that the first scout reported. Do not let the scouts talk with each other until each has made a scouting report to you and then get them together and see where they agree and disagree. It is better to have agreement after a scout reports than to have agreement before the scouting is done.

Final Hints and Special Drills

1. If a man is cutting for the basket, be sure to give him the proper lead.
2. Do not slap the ball in defensive territory.
3. Break up a stalling game before the opponents have an opportunity to organize it.
4. Set plays used against a man-to-man type of defense will not work as well against a sinking defense or against a roaming defense.
5. In retreating on defense, try to face the play.
6. If screened, take the screener.
7. On screen plays, loosen up and let your teammates through.
8. Use screen plays on a close-guarding team.
9. Drive against a pick-up defense.
10. It is hard to upset a good defensive team.
11. Build your offense first, then your defense.
12. You will maintain interest in fundamental drills if the boys see a reason for them.
13. Your fundamental drills should essentially be a part of your offense and defense.
14. A reward for fighting for a loose ball should at least be a fair and decent shot at the basket.

15. If the other team gets the loose balls, you are being outfought.
16. Play fast against a team that is not in condition.
17. Play aggressively and rush a mechanical team.
18. If a team does not have good long shots, loosen up on them and give them shots from the floor rather than permit them to get close in.
19. The spirit of the subs on the bench will influence the boys who are playing.
20. Have plenty of balls for practice, one ball for every two men.

SPLIT-VISION DRILL

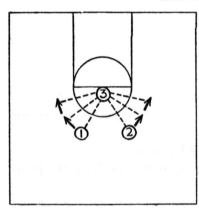

Chart 84. The purpose of this drill is to teach the pivot man to have as wide a range of vision as possible. Nos. 1 and 2 each have a ball. No. 1 passes. As soon as No. 3 catches it, No. 3 passes back to No. 1 and No. 2 passes in. The timing should be such that, as No. 3 passes, the ball is on its way from No. 2 to No. 3. No. 3 passes back to No. 2, and the ball is on on its way from No. 1 again. As the drill continues, Nos. 1 and 2 gradually work to the side as indicated in the diagram. This gives a wide area for No. 3 to watch.

PASSING DRILL

Chart 85. There are five offensive players and one defensive man, X. X tries to catch, bat, or touch the ball as it is passed. Offensive players cannot pass to man next to them. In other words, No. 1 must pass to No. 4 or No. 5. If to No. 5, then No. 5 must pass to No. 1 or No. 3. If X touches pass, he replaces the man who passed the ball. This teaches faking, quick floor passes, and speed in passing.

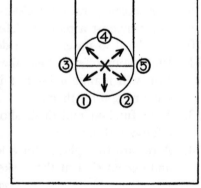

TIPPING DRILL

Chart 86. The foul shooter takes the shot. If he misses, the men under the basket try to tip it in. The player who succeeds becomes the next shooter. The first shooter takes his place under the hoop.

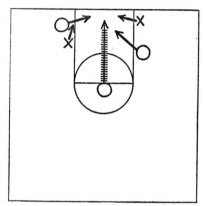

GUARD CRASHING DRILL NO. 1

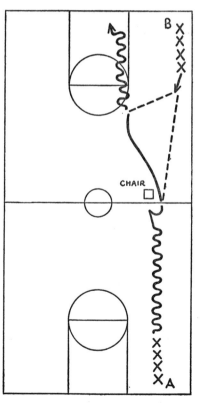

Chart 87. Line up players into A and B lines as indicated. Have the players in line A dribble hard to a position right in front of the chair. Before passing, player A uses a head and step fake to the inside and then passes to the outside to player in line B, who cuts out to meet the pass. Player A sidesteps around chair and, with terrific speed, cuts for the basket. Player B gives a pass to A, and A dribbles at full speed for lay-up shot. B follows shot and then lines up back of line A, while A lines up in back of line B.

GUARD CRASHING DRILL NO. 2

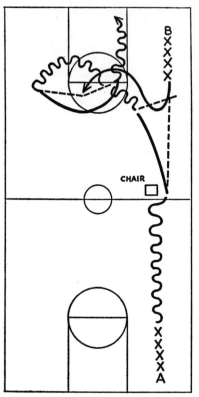

Chart 88. Line up players as indicated. Have the players in line A dribble hard to a position right in front of the chair. Before passing, player A uses a head and step fake to the inside and then passes to the outside to player in line B, who cuts out to meet the pass. Player A sidesteps around chair and, with terrific speed, cuts for the basket and receives pass from B. He dribbles across the floor as indicated, pivots, and passes to B, who has cut for pivot position. A cuts around B and again takes pass from him and dribbles in to the basket. B follows and then lines up in back of line A, while A lines up in back of line B.

GUARD CRASHING DRILL NO. 3

Chart 89. Line up players as indicated. A passes in to B, who comes to meet the pass. B dribbles to the position near the center of the free-throw line, pivots, and feeds pass to A, who has cut in lines indicated. A dribbles in for lay-up shot. B follows. A and B then exchange original positions.

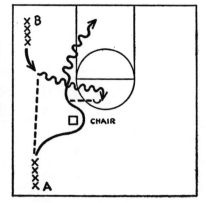

DRIBBLE AND CUTTING DRILL

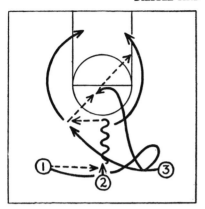

Chart 90. No. 1 passes to No. 2 and cuts over to screen for him. Meanwhile No. 2 dribbles in, passes to No. 3, and pivots toward basket. No. 3 passes to No. 4, who relays ball to No. 2 for lay-up shot.

GOING TO MEET PASS

Chart 91. Line up players as indicated. A passes to B who cuts to meet pass. A drives in line indicated around B, takes pass, and dribbles in for lay-up shot. A and B then exchange original positions.

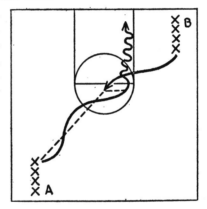

PASSING DRILLS

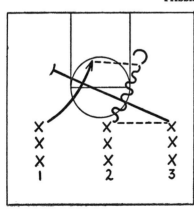

Chart 92. Line up players as indicated. No. 3 passs to No. 2 and cuts in front of No. 2 and across toward No. 1, screening for him. As soon as No. 3 passes No. 2, No. 2 dribbles fast in lines shown, pivots, and passes to No. 1, who is cutting for the basket. Check on all fundamentals. No. 3 goes to the end of line 1, No. 1 to line 2, and No. 2 to line 3.

PASSING DRILLS (Cont.)

Chart 93. Line up players as indicated. No. 1 passes to No. 2 and cuts for the basket in line shown. No. 2 passes high to No. 1, who takes it and shoots. No. 3 rebounds and dribbles away from the basket to the corner and makes a high hook pass to No. 1. No. 3 goes to end of line 1, No. 1 to line 2, and No. 2 to line 3.

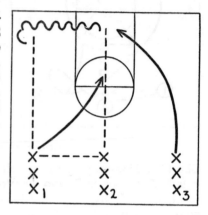

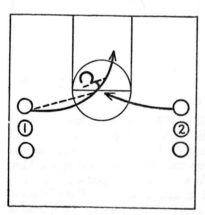

Chart 94. Line up players as indicated. No. 2 cuts for the pivot line and No. 1 gives him the pass. No. 2 takes one dribble, pivots, and passes to No. 1, who cuts behind. No. 2 then swings around and follows the shot. He picks up ball after No. 1 shoots for basket and passes out to another No. 1 man. The men change positions after each maneuver.

FAST-BREAK PASSING DRILL

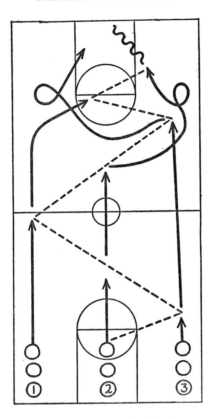

Chart 95. Line up players as indicated. No. 2 starts drill and passes to No. 3. No. 3 passes back to No. 2, and No. 2 passes to No. 1, who in turn passes back to No. 2. No. 2 passes to No. 3 and cuts behind him as No. 3 turns toward center and feeds ball to No. 1. No. 3 cuts behind No 1. No. 1 passes to No. 2, who has reversed. No. 2 takes one dribble and shoots. No. 3 and No. 1 follow. This drill teaches speed in running and ball handling and good change of direction. Players No. 2 and No. 3 need not use a change of direction move after No. 1 has received a pass at the free-throw line, depending largely on the timing desired. All three boys may go into the figure 8 weave.

DRIBBLE, PIVOT, AND PASS TO TRAILER

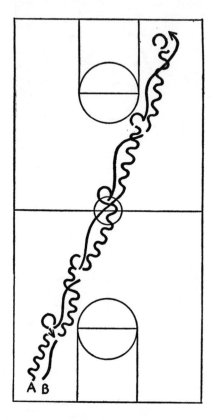

Chart 96. A dribbles about 20 feet, pivots to the left, and gives a short three-foot pass to B, who is a trailer. B then dribbles about 20 feet, pivots in the same direction, and gives the same pass to A, who has swung in behind B and now is the trailer. A then dribbles, and B swings in as trailer; this is continued until the players reach the other end of the court. Be sure to check on fundamentals of dribbling and pivoting. It is better to practice this slowly at first.

DRIBBLING DRILL

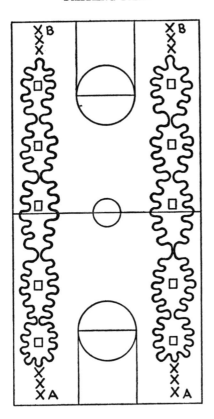

Chart 97. Line up players as shown. A starts drill. He dribbles up to chair with left hand, then changes ball to right hand and dribbles past and around the chair on right side. He continues to the next chair and goes around on the other side—using his left hand. Then he goes to the next chair, goes around it on the right side, and uses his right hand. He always uses the hand away from the chair to dribble past. When he gets to the opposite end of the floor, he passes to B, who brings the ball back in the same way.

PASSING AND CUTTING DRILL

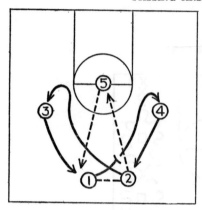

Chart 98. No. 1 passes to No. 2 and sets up a screen for him. No. 2 passes to No. 5. Nos. 1 and 2 both cut for basket. If either is open, No. 5 gives him the ball. If not, they turn out to forward positions, for the forwards No. 3 and No. 4 are now out in the original positions of Nos. 1 and 2. No. 5 passes to No. 3. No. 3 now passes to No. 4 and screens for him just as No. 1 did for No. 2. No. 4 passes to No. 5, and both Nos. 3 and 4 cut exactly as Nos. 1 and 2 did before. Nos. 1 and 2 are now coming out to their original positions. This is a good passing and cutting drill. The players like it, especially if Nos. 3 and 4 cut in to basket and one of them gets the pass from No. 5.

DRIBBLE, PIVOT, AND PASS

Chart 99. Each player dribbles, pivots, and passes to next man, as shown. He then takes the place of the man passed to.

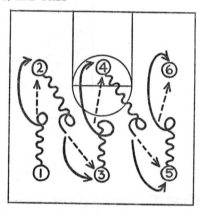

DRIBBLE, PIVOT, AND PASS

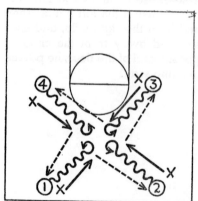

Chart 100. Either Nos. 1, 2, 3, or 4 starts drill by dribbling to center. Guard X tries to break up dribble. Upon reaching center, the dribbler pivots and passes to next man, as shown.

PASSING AND CUTTING DRILL

Chart 101. No. 1 passes to No. 2, while Nos. 4 and 5 come up to screen. No. 2 passes to No. 3, and both Nos. 1 and 2 cut to the basket. No. 3 feeds the free man.

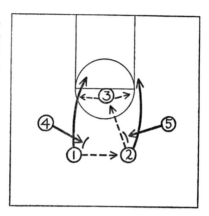

REBOUNDING DRILLS

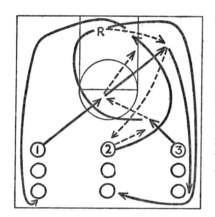

Chart 102. Line up players as indicated. No. 2 passes to No. 3 and drives around him, as No. 3 relays the ball to No. 1. As No. 1 feeds No. 2 under the basket, No. 3 cuts across for the rebound. The ball is passed to No. 1 near the corner, who throws it back to the next man in line 2. No. 1 goes to the end of line 3, No. 2 to line 1, and No. 3 to line 2.

Chart 103. Line up players as shown. No. 2 passes to No. 3 and goes straight in for the rebound. No. 3 relays to No. 1, who shoots. No. 2 whips the ball to No. 3 near corner, and the latter fires it back to the next man in the feeding line. No. 1 goes to end of line 3, No. 2 to line 1, and No. 3 to line 2.

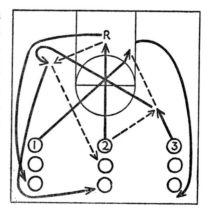

SHOOTING OVER SCREENER

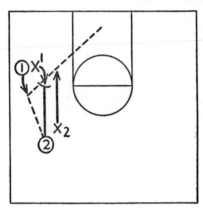

Chart 104. No. 2 passes in to No. 1, who comes out to meet pass. No. 2 then goes on inside of No. 1 to screen. X2 follows No. 2 so that there is no shift in the defensive men. No. 1 uses No. 2 as a screen and shoots over him.

Chart 105. No. 2 passes to No. 1, who meets pass. No. 2, with terrific speed, cuts as if to go around No. 1 and X1. X2, figuring that No. 2 is trying for the guard-around play, decides to cut back of X1 and pick up No. 2 on his way to the basket. No. 2 stops in front of No. 1, who hands him the ball. Using No. 1 as a screen, No. 2 shoots over him. Remember that in both Charts 104 and 105 we are shooting from one of our spots (see Chart 1, page 38).

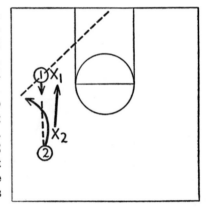

SPECIAL POSITION PLAYS

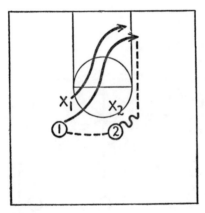

Chart 106. Offensive player No. 1 passes to No. 2 and then cuts for the basket, trying to get position on the defensive player X1. No. 2 takes one dribble and passes to No. 1 just as he arrives near the basket. No. 1 then takes a shot.

SPECIAL POSITION PLAYS (Cont.)

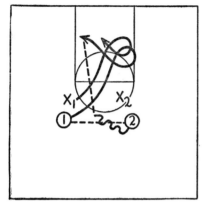

Chart 107. No. 1 passes to No. 2 and cuts for the basket. He uses a change of direction to throw off X1. No. 2 takes a dribble back in the direction from which No. 1 had originally passed to him. He then passes to No. 1.

Index

A.A.U. Tournament, 141–143
Accuracy in passing, 29, 101
Action, styles of, to please spectators, 94
Adequate staffs, advantage to coach, 197
Adjusting the ball, right-handed passers, 31
Advancing the ball, fast breaks, 51
Afternoon practice, 4
Aggressiveness, 65–85, 144
Alabama, 15
All-Star games, 23
Ankles, care of, 5
Arch of shot, amount of, 41
Arm muscles, development of, 9
Assignments:
  by speed or size, 148
  changes of during time out, 172–173
  offensive, 66
Athlete's foot, treatment of, 5
Athletes, mental conditioning of, 179
Athletic director, duty of, 189
Attack strategy:
  pivot play, 17
  planning during game, 196
  quick-breaking, 17

Attendance, estimate of at basketball, 14
Averages, increase in scoring, 95

Backboard rebounds, control of, 125
Back-court play by guards, 126
Backhand pass, 33
Back screens, 147
Balance formations, side, 114
Balance, player, 140
Ball fake, 59
Ball handling:
  routine, 166
  unnecessary, 61
"Ball-Hawks," 130
Ball, position of before play, 92
Ball possession, 28
  capitalizing on, 23
  assignment at center-jump, 68
Balls:
  checking air pressure of, 189
Balm, use of, 5
Banking shots, 37
Baseball pass, use of, 91
Base line, moving out from, 90
Basic Formations, Kentucky, 121–122

Basketball, evolution of, 139
Basketball systems, comparsion with football, 15
Batting the ball, 149
Beatty, Pakenham, 3
Becker, Moe, 18
Bed-rule, 2
Bee, Coach Clair, 18
Beverages, types best for training diet, 186
Bird, Jerry, 42
Blind shots, objections to, 66
Blisters, treatment of, 5
Blocking of shots, 126
Blood pressure, checking, 4
Bluffing a shot, 126
Body balance, tip-off to defenseman, 126
Body fake, right, use of, 59
Body faking, 147
Body protection in dribbling, 52
Boric acid, use of, 7
Bounce, height of, in dribbles, 51
Bounce pass:
  reason for, 29
  two-handed, 29
Boxer's stance, use of, 128
Boxing players, 124
Bragging about players, avoidance of, 195
Breads, use of, on day of game, 186
Breaking down center of floor, 97
Break-throughs on tip-off, 130
Bringing ball out to free-throw line, 161
Broken blisters, treatment of, 5
Brush screens, creating, 110
Burrow, Bob, 42–48

Calvert, Gerry, 42
Canvas traveling bags, reasons not used, 190
Carelessness of players, 171
Cassady, Bill, 42
Catching the ball, position while, 29
Cautious playing, advantages of, 166
Celtics, the Original, 15, 17
Center, best physical characteristics of, 89
Center-jump, 64
  elimination of, 142
Center, keeping lane open, 101
Center line, advancing over, 101
Center:
  mechanics of pivot play, 90
  position in zone defense, 153
  stance at jump, 64

Chalk-talks:
  during practice, 183
  pre-game, 176
Championship basketball, 1, 2
Chance shots, avoidance of, 92
Change-of-direction turns, 57
Change of pace, 68
Charging, 126
Charging opponents, protecting the ball from, 89
Chartman, use of, 65
Chest-pass, two-handed, 29
Citizenship, building, 193
Circles, running in, 103
Classes, attendance at, 185
Cleanliness, teaching, 4
Clearing space for teammates, 101
Close shooting, necessity for practice, 36
Coaches:
  advice to beginners, 174
  general rules for, 10, 11, 12
  treatment of players, 193
Coach-to-player relationship, 192
  understanding of material, 171
Coffee, use of, by players, 186
Cold packs, use of, 5
Colds, prevention of, 7
Combination defense styles, 150–151
Competitive instinct, 13
Complete offense, building up, 103
Concentration while shooting, 41
Conditioning, 1, 2, 24, 25
Confidence:
  between teammates, 69
  instillation of, 22
Conservative game, playing, 195
Contact, relation in screening, 70
Continuity plays, effectiveness of, 119
Continuity practice, 119
Control of game by substitution, 171
Coordination requirements, 86, 87
Corners, keeping out of, 101
Covering opponents, man-to-man, 145
Crashing on tip-off plays, 168
Credit, awarding proper, 192
Crip shots, 45
Crisscross pattern, 98–99
Crisscross screen, two players, 73
Criticism of individual players between halves, 195
Critiques:
  coaches and players, 149
  during time-out, 173
Cross-arm shot, 47
Cross steps, avoidance of, 128

Crouch, use of, 68
Cursing, avoidance of, 193
Cut off of pivot man, 92
Cutting drill, with diagrams, 211
Cutting for the basket, 99
Cutting in five-man offense, 120
Cutting off a side-dribble, 167
Cutting off plays around pivot man, 151
Cutting the squad, 12
Cutting under basket, 45
Cutting, use of middle lane, 120

Danger zones, how to get out of, 149
Data, compilation of, on opponents, 197
Dayton, 15
Dead stops, how to use, 54
Deception, 28
Decoy play, 18, 19
Decoys, use of, 18
Defense:
  advantage of practice, 142
  after shot, 148
  against double screen on pivot man,
    168
  against free-throws, 169
  against held-ball play, with diagrams,
    169
  against side screen, 167
  against tall centers, 146
  against tip-off, 168
  dominant types of, 1917-1928, 140
  getting set for, 96
  principles, 133–138
Defense man:
  change of direction, 166
  clearing, 62
  control of rebound against two oppo-
    nents, 166–167
  drawing out, 59
  impeding, 70
  outmaneuvering by pivot, 92
  screen play against, 73
Defense men, loosening of, 60
Defense plays, effective, 116
Defense weakness, 142
Defenses, diagrams of, 116
Defensive aggressiveness, 85
Defensive assignments, diagrammed,
    148
Defensive basket, moving ball away,
    50
Defensive dribbling, 50
Defensive faking, 60
Defensive free-throw, fast break, 98

Defensive guard with ball after re-
    bound, 166, 167
Defensive hints, 128, 129, 130
Defensive play, best time to teach, 87,
    88
Defensive players, blocking of, 56
Defensive review of opponents' plays,
    183
Defensive styles:
  man-to-man, 16
  screen-switch, 16, 17
  zone, 16
Defensive tip-off, when to play, 64
Degrading of players in public, avoid-
    ance of, 194
Dehnert, Dutch, 17
Demonstrations by coach, 10
Depth of position, 144
Designed areas, shooting from, 39
Desire to win, importance of, 2
Destroying team work, 23
Details, mastery of, 85
Diagnosis of opponents' play, 166
Diagonal drive, shot to terminate, 46
Diathermy, use of, 6
Diet control in high school players, 185
Diet, supervision of, 184
Direct paths to basket, blocking, 148
Discipline, 174
Disinfectants, use of, 6
Diversion of players away from home,
    176
Diving on loose balls, 65
Double-screen, defense against, with dia-
    grams, 168
Drawing up defense men by faking, 59
Dress of team while traveling, 176
Dressing at hotel in tournament play,
    176
Dribble drill, with diagrams, 204
Dribble-in shots, one-handed, 45
Dribbler, driving to sidelines, 56
Dribblers, forcing man to pivot, 167
Dribbling:
  back-court, 125
  by pivot man, 93
  objections to, 56
  offensive, by guards, 88
  proper use of, 54
  short, 55
  technique, 55
Dribbling down center, diagram of play,
    100
Dribbling drills, pivot and pass, with
    diagrams, 208, 209, 210

Drills against fast breaks, 161, 162
Drive under basket, shot for, 46
Duquesne, 20, 21
Duties of players, discussed, 87

Early scoring, psychological effect of, 195
Easy games, mental approach to, 171
Eating, amount of before tournaments, 180
Education:
  basketball as an aid to, 193
  use of trips as part of, 175
Edwards, Leroy, 76, 77
Elbows, position of, in passing, 29
Eligibility, checking, 12
Emergencies, use of time out for, 172
Energy conservation, defense for, 158
English, how to secure, 41
Equipment:
  carrying of, 174
  clean, need for, 174
  collection of, after game, 190
  last-minute adjustment of, 195
  packing of uniforms, 189
  practice, 4
  supervision of by student manager, 189
Errors, opponents', 62
Escape from pressing defense, 51
Evans, Billy, 18
Exercises, 23
Experience, enlarging of by coach, 10
Experimenting by substitution, 170
Extra uniforms, packing for trips, 190

Facing the play, 201
Fading to cover offense men, 59
Fake injuries as strategy, 58, 59
Fake passes, use of, 59
Faking, 58, 59
Falls on the floor, 59
False footwork, elimination of, 59
Fans, keeping away from team before tournaments, 179
Fast ball versus deliberate games, 85
Fast break:
  after missed free-throw, 100
  after successful free-throw, 101
  as scoring threat, 96, 97
  defense against, 160, 161
Fast-break passing drills, with diagrams, 207
Fast breaks:
  patterns for, 97

Fatigue:
  cumulative, 24
  substitution because of, 171
Favorites, avoiding, 11
Feeder man, use of, 92, 93
Feet:
  care of, 5, 6
  position of, for passing, 40, 41
  toughening of, 5
Feinting opponents out of position, 62
Fighting for ball, 145
Fighting spirit, stimulation of, 194
Figure-eight plays, 120
Finances, limitations on scouting, 197
Finger snap in passing, 30
Fingers:
  position of, at center jump, 64
  position of, in catching low pass, 29
First team, composition of, 13
Five-man continuities, 119
Five-man figure-eight play, 121
Flat-footed play, avoidance of, 124
Flexibility of plays, 87
Flip pass, 32
Flip shot, 47
Float passes, 147
Floor burns, treatment of, 5
Floor direction by guards, 103
Floor play, offensive, 165
Floors, standard size, 156
Florida, University of, 178
Follow-through in shooting, 44
Foot fakes, 59
Footwork, 59, 60
  of pivot man, 91
  tip-offs, 124
Forcing retreats, 162
Forcing shots by defense, 124
Forcing the shooter away from basket, 47
Forcing the shot, 126
Forward, reversing without ball, 61
Forwards:
  defensive play of, 140
  footwork of, 59
  how to step out in advancing, 60
  methods of faking by, 58
  physical characteristics of, 87
  position of, 60
  reversing, 60
Fouling, times most prevalent, 165
Fouling, prevention of, 136
Fouling out, danger of, in first half, 171
Fouls, accumulation of, 170
Fouls, first half, 171

Freak shots, 51
Free balls, 65
Freedom systems, 86
Freeing a man, offensive, 92
Free-throw line:
plays from, 169
setting up pivots on, 90
Free-throw missed, fast break, 100
Free-throws, time allotted to practice of, 183
Freezing the ball, 165
Freshmen as student managers, 189
Fried foods, avoidance of by players, 188
Fruits, types best suited for players, 186
Fumbling, causes of, 33
Fundamental shot, 37
Fungicidal powder, use of, 5

Game-play, correction of, during time-out, 172, 173
Game, progress of, 195
Game strategy, 18
Games:
beginning time of, 174
spacing of, 181
Gauze, use of, over blisters, 6
Generalship by coach, 195
Getting position, definition, 146
Give and go style, 15
Goal shooting, 35
distance for practice, 37
position for left forward, 37
Going down on plays, guards, 126
Grawemeyer, Phil, 42
Guard across play, with diagrams, 75
Guard-around plays, 103
Guard crashing drills, with diagrams, 203, 204
Guard fundamental offense drill, 93
Guard offense, fundamental drill, 22
Guard offense, fundamental practice time for, 183
Guard playing two opponents, 126, 127, 162
Guard, position on play from center, 124
Guarding against screens, 73
Guarding man after pass, 124
Guarding man with ball, 128
Guarding man without ball, 128
Guarding opponents' first move, 148
Guarding the pivot man, 146, 147
Guards:
best physical characteristics for, 87

Guards *(cont.)*:
deception of, 59
footwork, 124
general rules for, 128, 129
methods of faking by, 58
offensive requirements for, 102, 103
part of in offense, 88
position of on defense, 123

Habits, avoidance of teaching bad, 25
Hands, position of, for receiving pass, 91
Harassment, 127
Hard passes, avoiding, 28
Harmony, need for, 23
Hats for players, 8
Hatton, Vernon, 17, 42
Head fake, 58
Height, advantages of tall centers, 89
Height of ball, gauging by center, 64
Held balls, 65
Hernia, checking for, 5
High jump, use of, in dribble-in shots, 45
High passes to centers, 92
Holding the ball, 41
Hook pass, 32
Hope shots, danger of, 171
Hurrying the offense man, 127

Ideal combinations for guards, 88
Index finger, position of, in passes, 41
Individual abilities, use of, 98
Individual defense play, 123
Individual glory, discouraging of, 23
Individual responsibilities, 68, 69
Individual skill, practice, 22
Individual stars, building a team with, 23
Influenza shots, use of, 4, 7
Information, furnishing from bench by substitution, 195
Initial passer, tying up, 160
Inner-socks, use of, 4
Inside positions on defense, 126
Interceptions, 127
Interference, running after pivot, 57
Iowa, 15
Irritability of players, cause of, 8

Jealousy among players, 193
Judgment, necessity for, in pivot-men, 91
Judgment of distance, how to improve, 35

Julian, Alvin, 26
Jump turn around shot, 47
Jumping, defense men, 126
Jumping ropes, use of, 9
Jumping, take-off for shots, 126

Kentucky, University of, team averages, 141, 142
Keogan, Dr. George, 16
Kleenex, use of, on trips, 190
Knees, position of, for recovery after jumps, 64

Lambert, Coach Ward, 17
Lateral passing under basket, 34
Lateral screen, establishing of, 167
Lay-up shots:
    drills to increase speed of, 121
    examples of, 166
Lead, allowing sufficient, 34
Lead passes, 122
Leadership, building of, 193
Leaving a position, footwork, 61
Left forward:
    floor position in practice, 36, 37
    position in games, with diagrams, 38, 39
Left shoulder pass, 31
Left shoulder shot, 47
Leg muscles, development of, 9
Leg spring, 148
Lightness on feet, 65
Limitation of shifts, 145
Living quarters for players, 184
Loafing, 146
Loafing on recoveries, remedy for, 171
Locker-room speeches, 194
Long Island University, 18
Long shots:
    practice for guards, 88
    when to avoid, 35
Loose balls:
    picking up, 65
    possession by opponents, 202
Loosening the defenseman, 60
Low passes to center, 92

Man-to-man defense, 139, 140, 144
Man-to-man defense, adaptability, 150
Married players, problems of, 184
Managers:
    junior, 189
    refereeing for outside schools, 190
    study of rules by, 13
Matching men, 159

Meals while on trips, 176
Medicine balls in exercising, 9
Medical examinations, desirability of, 4
Medium shots, use of, 120
Mental approach to tournament play, 178
Mental guarding, 128
Merthiolate, use of, 5
Miscellaneous diet suggestions, 188
Misleading the opponent, 58
Mississippi, University of, 178
Mistakes, pointed out by coach, 195
Mixture of styles, 96
Modern versus old-style play, discussion of, 95, 96
Monopoly of play by individuals, 23
Morale, injury to, by fouling out, 171
Mouth, washing out before game, 194
Movement of defense men, how to interrupt, 70
Moving, waiting for right opportunity, 68

Naismith, Dr. James, 16
Narrow floors:
    best defenses on, 159
    plays adaptable to, 156
National Invitation Tournament, 96
NCAA Tournament, 166
NCAB, 36
Night clubs, team entertainment, 177
Night practice, desirability of, 4
Notes on individual players, 149
Numbers, getting advantage of, 61, 62

Off-balance, shooting when, 35
Offense and defense combinations, 142
Offense:
    duties of center after jump, 89
    five-man (see also Give and go style), 98, 99
    how to slow, 125
    individual, 67
    mechanical, 90, 91
    principles, 77–83
    proper attitude toward, 68
    three-man, 66
    two-man, 107
Offensive development, history of, 142
Offensive drills against tight defense, 182
Offensive men, outmaneuvering guards, 124
Offensive practice, 143
Offensive teams, hints for advancing, 99

Off-nights by brilliant players, remedy for, 171
One-handed shots, 44
One-two stops, use of, 56
One-two-two shifting zone defense, 156
Openings for shots by pivot man, 93
Opponents:
    cataloguing of, 68, 69
    cooling down, 172
    defenses of, 120
Option of passes, offense plays, 110
Organized attacks, discouraging by fast break, 96
Organized offenses, working through, 96
Outguessing the opposition, 68
Outlet passes, 96
Outlying men, covering at free-throw, 9
Out-of-bounds plays:
    defense moves, 128
    behind basket, 114
    side, 115
Outside area, passing to, 28
Outside shots, 19
Over-anxiety, effect of, on mistakes, 194
Over-coaching, 10
Over-eating on trips, 180
Overhead pass:
    one-handed, 31
    two-handed, 31
Overhead shot, two-handed, 44
Overloading the defense zone, 159
Over-shifting, dangers of, 159
Overwork, danger of, 1, 2

Paper cups, use of, 190
Parallel play, 59
Parents, distribution of schedules to, 176
Pass-and-cut tactics, best defense against, 159
Pass, high, 91
Passes:
    going out to meet, diagrams, 205
    moving forward to meet, 68, 69
    use of, instead of dribbles, 51
Pass-outs, length of, 93
Pass receiving, 29
Passing, 27–34
    diagonal, 28
    fake, 59
    general rules for, 27
    importance of timing in, 28
    to pivot man, 92
    types of, 28
    unnecessary, 61

Passing drills, use of, 12
Passing hints, 33, 34
Passing drills with diagrams, 202, 205
Patience in coaching, 10
Peak conditioning, early season, 4
Percentage game after free-throws, 96
Personal fouls, reducing number of, 159
Pettit, Bob, 18
Physical fitness for tournament play, 178
Picking-up opponents on defense, 144
Pick-up defense, 127
Pivot, front, 56
Pivoting, 54–57
Pivot man:
    defense man playing behind, 166
    getting proper position, 90
    requirements for, 90
    switching of, 120
Pivot offense, 99
Pivot play, general rules for, 90
Pivot position, substitution of forwards in emergency, 87
Pivot, reverse, 55
Pivot, side-line, 56
Plan of defense, pre-game discussions of, 194
Planned entertainment, value of, on trips, 177
Planning for second half, 195
Planning plays for a year, 11
Players:
    crouch position of, 68
    mornings off while traveling, 177
    qualifications of, in team play, 86, 87
    specialization of, 11, 12
    temperaments of, revealed by scouting, 199
Player-to-player relationship, 192
Playing away by opponents, 120
Playing close, guards, 123
Playing faults, when to correct, 9
Playing styles:
    California, 16
    eastern, 15, 18
    mid-west, 15
    southern, 71
Playing the ball, 140
Playing to the side, 147, 148
Plays:
    continuous, 121–122
    double screen, 76
    guard across, 75
    need for, 25, 26

Plays (cont.):
  numbering of, 86
  out-of-bounds, 113, 114
  patterns of, 61
  pre-game selection of, 195
  saving for second half, 195
  switching, 123
  to avoid telegraphing, 73
  types necessary for team, 93
  types siutable with one good man
      only, 156, 157
Polish, how to achieve, 62
Popular defenses, 154–155
Position of guards on defense, 128
Position, preventing opponents securing,
      160
Positive blocks, 145–150
Possession game, 121
Possession of the ball, 63–66, 128
Potassium permanganate solution, direc-
      tions for preparing, 5
Potential scorers, 98
Powder, drying, 5
Practice:
  best times for, 4
  defensive, 143
  early-season, 12, 13
  first week of, 12
  pre-season night, 4
  scrimmages, 13
  variation of, 183
Pre-game practice on opponent's floor,
      177
Pre-game team handling, 193
Pressure defense, 120
Pressure on offense men, 127
Prevention of shots, 127
Pride, injury of, 193
Principles of defense, 133–138
Principles of offense, 77–83
Proper leads, giving to man cutting, 201
Protecting the basket, 161
Protection for pivotman, 91
Publicity, danger of, 192
Purdue University, 17
Pushing the ball when dribbling, 51
Push-shot:
  in motion, 46
  two-handed, 45
Push-ups, 9

"Quarterbacking" by guards, 88
Quick breaks, value of, 60
Quick stops, trapping defense with, 124

Rallys, calling time outs in, 172

Ramsey, Frank, 17
Rebound control, practice time, 65
Rebounding drills, 211
Rebounding game, when effective, 160
Rebounds:
  control of, by guards, 88
  control of on free-throws, 169
  getting possession, 65
  under defense basket, 125
Regular meals, advantage of, 4
Relaxation while traveling, 176
Releasing potential pass-receivers, 34
Reorganizing when opponent rallys, 172
Reports, individual, by scouts, 199
Responsibility, individual, 148
Rest, effect on efficiency, 2
Resting on floor, danger of time-outs
      for, 172
Retreating defense, 144
Return passes, 32
Reversing, 147
Rewards for fighting for loose ball, 202
Rhode Island fast break, 96
Right forward, shooting position, with
      diagrams, 38, 39
Right-hand passing, 31
Right-of-way, defense man when cutting,
      167
Right shoulder pass, 31
Right shoulder shot, 47
Rollins, Kenneth, 25, 149
Roll pass, one-handed, 33
Room checks on overnight trips, 191
Rooming lists, preparation of, 176
Routines:
  breaking up of, 181
  establishing of, for traveling, 176, 177
  pre-tournament, 179
Running, 59
Running forward, early days, 87
Running through a defense, 150

Safety defense man, position after
      missed free-throw, 100
Sale, Aggie, 48
Salicylic acid, use of, 6
Sandwiching ball handler, 166
Schedule:
  tournament play, 179, 180
  traveling, 176
  for week of practice, 181
  mimeographing of, 176
School examinations, interruption of
      practice by, 181
Schools, visiting of opponents', 176

Score cards for fans, 19, 20
Scoring chances, individual, 67
Scoring threats, fast break, 95
Scouting, 18
Scouting bureaus, use of, 197
Scouting forms, use of, 198
Scouting notes, discussion of, 183
Scouting, personal, 197
Scouting reports, agreement between several, 200
Screen play, 124
  back, 75
  inside, 74
Screen plays:
  action of defense guard in, 128
  analysis of, 73–75
  defense against, 128
  legality of, 71
  types of, 70, 71
Scrimmages, referees for, 189, 190
Second team in practice, 144
Sectional highlights of play, 15
Selection of food, range of, 187
Self-control, practice of, 194
Selfishness in dribbling, 52
Semi-circle, avoidance in practice shooting, 36
Series plays, for guards, 102
Seton Hall, 19
Set plays:
  against man-to-man defense, 201
  defense against, 128
Setting defense at center-line, 143
Shifting, 145, 146
Shifting man-to-man defense, 150, 151
Shifting of opponents by defense men, 150
Shifting zones, 140
Shin injuries, taping of, 6
Shin splints, use of, 6
Shirts, colored, 189
Shoes:
  dusting of, 5
  use of, in practice and in game, 190
Shooting, 35–49
  diagrams of positions, 38–39
  "Give and go," 15
  long shots by guards, 88
  one-handed, 15
  over screener, best time for practicing, 182
  when not to, 35, 36
Shooting drills:
  diagrams for, 212
  necessity for, 183

Shooting hints, 51
Short shot game, 55
Short shots, best defense against, 158
Short steps, use on defense, 128
Shortening steps, 62
Shots:
  arch of, 43
  follow-up after, 69
  medium length, 120
Showers, use of, 8
Side-line play, centers, 90
Sidelines, best pass from, 32
Side-screen, defense against, with diagrams, 167
Side-stepping, 126
Simplifying patterns, 93
Sinking defense, 144
Sinking man-to-man defense, 151
Size of squad, 12
Slap pass, 32
Sleep, amount of in tournament play, 180
Slide dribble, 92, 149
Slow set styles, use of continuities, 119
Small guards on tall centers, 147
Smoking, 2
Smothering, plays for, 167
Socks, type of, 4
Sore feet, treatment of, 5
Sound offenses, 96
Southeastern Conference tournaments, 161, 178
Spastic condition of muscles, 6
Special position plays, 212
Specific areas, guarding of, 153
Spectator appreciation of defense, 143, 144
Spectators, advice for, 14, 15, 16
Spectators' interest, 95
Speed in team play, 84, 85, 103
Speed passing, practice of, 194
Spin on ball in passing, 29
Spirit of play by substitutes, 202
Splitting two opponents, play for, 168
Split-vision, 59
Split-vision drills, with diagram, 202
Sponge, use of, to cushion injured feet, 5
Sports writers, relation to team, 192
Spot shooting, typical schedule for practicing, 182
Sprains, treatment of, 6
Spread of zone defense, 158
Spur-of-the-moment plays, 96
Staleness, 8, 9

Stall game 119, 141
Stall plays, 120
Stalling games, weaknesses of, 165
Stamina, building of, 119
Stance for shooting, 40, 43
Stance of pivot man, 91
Standing guard, early players, 88
Stars, guarding individual, 166
Starting line-up, resting of, before game starts, 194
Stationary defense, 142
Statistics, analysis to aid offense, 65
Stealing the ball, 53
Step-in shot, description, 47
St. Louis, 15
Stops, sudden, 54, 55
Straight lines, running in, 62
Strategy (*see* Attack strategy)
Striking of players by coach, avoidance of, 193
Student manager, duties of, 189
Study, importance of good grades, 193
Studying opponents' style, 62
Studying while on road trips, 176
Style of play, University of Kentucky, 144
Substitution:
  control by, 12, 19
  for man with four fouls, 171
  importance of timeliness, 195
Substitutions, when to make, 171
Success, achievement, of, 193
Sulfa ointment, use of, 5
Superior ball handling, 144
Supervision, danger of too-close, 191
Sweat socks, amount to carry on trips, 190
Sweat suits, use of, 5
Switching, definition, 163
Switching of men, dangers inherent in, 150–151
Synchronization of passes, 90

Talking on the floor, 127
Tannic acid, use in foot treatment, 5
Taping:
  methods of, on injured feet, 7
  when to do, 194
Teaching ability of coach, 8
Team defense:
  early methods, 139
  theory of, 145
Team in motion, 98
Team patterns, advantage of scouting, 160–161

Team play:
  first steps, 22, 23
  general principles, 85, 86
Teams:
  off-floor association, 192
  watching tournament games when not playing, 179
Teamwork in defense, 142–143
Telephones, blocking off during tournaments, 180
Temper, control of, by coach, 193
Temperatures proper for games, 7
Ten-second rule, 142
Tension, relieving for shooter, 43
Territory, leaving uncovered, 125
Theatres, use of, in entertainment, 177
Theory of play, and new coach, 93
Three-lane fast break, 153
Three-men continuities, 119
Three-second rule, 72, 146
Three-two shifting zone defense, 153
Three-two zone defense, plays against, 117
Tight defense, practicing against, time for, 182
Time factor on trips, 177
Time-outs:
  general rules for, 172
  utilization of, 172
Timing of passes to pivot, 90
Tincture of benzion, proper use of, 5
Tip-in baskets, 48
Tip-off play, center, 115
Tipping drills, with diagrams, 202
Tip shot, 48
Tiredness (*see* Fatigue)
Tonsils, diseased, 4
Tournament play, factors governing, 178
Tournament sites, when to reach, 179
Tournament squads, handling of, 179
Tournaments, pre-game resting, 179
Tradition, its use in training, 1
Trailers, position after missed free-throw, 100
Trainers, preparation for trips, 190
Training, 1, 2
Training tables, need for, 184
Traveling bags for players, 190
Triangle formation, use in tip-offs, 168
Trips, organization of, 174
Tsioropoulos, Lou, 18
Turn around shots, one-handed, 46
Turning and pivoting, 55
Two-handed overhead shot, 44

Two-handed push shot, 40
Two-handed underhand shot, 41
Two-one-two shifting zone defense, 155
Two-three shifting zone defense, 155
Two-timing on defense, 167
Two-timing weak players, 150
Two-two-one shifting zone, 157

Unbalanced position, finishing dribble
   in, 55
Under basket shots, 45
Underhand pass:
   one-handed, 30
   two-handed, 30
Underhand shot, two-handed, 41
Uniformity in passes, 85
Uniforms, proper, 4
Units, operation of, 98
Unselfishness in shots, 51
Upsets in tournament play, 178

Vegetables, types best for training, 186
Versatility of players, 11
Viewpoints of spectators, importance
   to coach, 161
Visitors during tournament period, 179
Vitamin pills, use of, 84

Waistline, passing to, 34
Walks, use as relaxation, 177
Wandering, avoidance of, 68
Warm-up drills, 9
Warm-ups, watching your opponents',
   195
Washing between halves, 196
Watching passer after pass, 127

Watching the opponent, importance of,
   149
Watson, Bobby, 17
Weaknesses, spotting of, 61, 62, 196
Weaving patterns, 98
Weight charts, 7
Weight, fluctuation of, 7
Well-wishers, troubles caused by, 180
Whitfield's Ointment, use of, 5
Whittaker, Skippy, 18
Widowitz, Paul, 19
Winning combinations, breaking up, 171
Winning early games, necessity of, 2
Withholding the ball from play, 27
Wraps, muslin, for ankles, 5
Wrist snap in shooting, 43

X-rays, use of, 6

Y-formation on defense, 169
Yates, George, 48
Yelling, use of, in deception, 127

Zone defense:
   diagrams, 158
   making opponent come out, 120
   methods of breaking, 120
   origination of, 140
   period of greatest effectiveness, 141
   plays against, 116
   principles of, 153
   shifting, 141
   strong points of, 158
   weakness inherent in, 159
   with fast break, 97